C-4895 CAREER EXAMINATION SERIES

This is your
PASSBOOK for...

Maintenance Supervisor I, II (Building)

Test Preparation Study Guide
Questions & Answers

NATIONAL LEARNING CORPORATION®

COPYRIGHT NOTICE

This book is SOLELY intended for, is sold ONLY to, and its use is RESTRICTED to individual, bona fide applicants or candidates who qualify by virtue of having seriously filed applications for appropriate license, certificate, professional and/or promotional advancement, higher school matriculation, scholarship, or other legitimate requirements of education and/or governmental authorities.

This book is NOT intended for use, class instruction, tutoring, training, duplication, copying, reprinting, excerption, or adaptation, etc., by:

1) Other publishers
2) Proprietors and/or Instructors of "Coaching" and/or Preparatory Courses
3) Personnel and/or Training Divisions of commercial, industrial, and governmental organizations
4) Schools, colleges, or universities and/or their departments and staffs, including teachers and other personnel
5) Testing Agencies or Bureaus
6) Study groups which seek by the purchase of a single volume to copy and/or duplicate and/or adapt this material for use by the group as a whole without having purchased individual volumes for each of the members of the group
7) Et al.

Such persons would be in violation of appropriate Federal and State statutes.

PROVISION OF LICENSING AGREEMENTS – Recognized educational, commercial, industrial, and governmental institutions and organizations, and others legitimately engaged in educational pursuits, including training, testing, and measurement activities, may address request for a licensing agreement to the copyright owners, who will determine whether, and under what conditions, including fees and charges, the materials in this book may be used them. In other words, a licensing facility exists for the legitimate use of the material in this book on other than an individual basis. However, it is asseverated and affirmed here that the material in this book CANNOT be used without the receipt of the express permission of such a licensing agreement from the Publishers. Inquiries re licensing should be addressed to the company, attention rights and permissions department.

All rights reserved, including the right of reproduction in whole or in part, in any form or by any means, electronic or mechanical, including photocopying, recording, or by any information storage and retrieval system, without permission in writing from the Publisher.

Copyright © 2024 by
National Learning Corporation

212 Michael Drive, Syosset, NY 11791
(516) 921-8888 • www.passbooks.com
E-mail: info@passbooks.com

PASSBOOK® SERIES

THE *PASSBOOK® SERIES* has been created to prepare applicants and candidates for the ultimate academic battlefield – the examination room.

At some time in our lives, each and every one of us may be required to take an examination – for validation, matriculation, admission, qualification, registration, certification, or licensure.

Based on the assumption that every applicant or candidate has met the basic formal educational standards, has taken the required number of courses, and read the necessary texts, the *PASSBOOK® SERIES* furnishes the one special preparation which may assure passing with confidence, instead of failing with insecurity. Examination questions – together with answers – are furnished as the basic vehicle for study so that the mysteries of the examination and its compounding difficulties may be eliminated or diminished by a sure method.

This book is meant to help you pass your examination provided that you qualify and are serious in your objective.

The entire field is reviewed through the huge store of content information which is succinctly presented through a provocative and challenging approach – the question-and-answer method.

A climate of success is established by furnishing the correct answers at the end of each test.

You soon learn to recognize types of questions, forms of questions, and patterns of questioning. You may even begin to anticipate expected outcomes.

You perceive that many questions are repeated or adapted so that you can gain acute insights, which may enable you to score many sure points.

You learn how to confront new questions, or types of questions, and to attack them confidently and work out the correct answers.

You note objectives and emphases, and recognize pitfalls and dangers, so that you may make positive educational adjustments.

Moreover, you are kept fully informed in relation to new concepts, methods, practices, and directions in the field.

You discover that you are actually taking the examination all the time: you are preparing for the examination by "taking" an examination, not by reading extraneous and/or supererogatory textbooks.

In short, this PASSBOOK®, used directedly, should be an important factor in helping you to pass your test.

MAINTENANCE SUPERVISOR I, II (BUILDING)

DUTIES:
As a **Maintenance Supervisor I (Building),** you would supervise the maintenance, repair, operation, construction, and reconstruction of buildings and equipment at all facilities within a division including the electrical, mechanical, heating, ventilating, air conditioning, and water and wastewater treatment systems. You would plan and estimate major repair and construction projects including materials and work schedules. You would use automated computer systems in the performance of your duties.

As a **Maintenance Supervisor II (Building),** you would plan, direct, and evaluate the supervision of maintenance, repair, operation, construction, and reconstruction of buildings and equipment at all facilities within a division including the preventive maintenance program. You would plan and direct the operation and installation of electrical, mechanical, heating, ventilating, air conditioning, and water and wastewater treatment systems; estimate the extent of major repair projects and required materials; and prepare periodic reports of maintenance and repair programs and condition reports of equipment and systems. You would also oversee and ensure the maintenance of security systems and safety procedures for Thruway facilities and equipment. You would use automated computer systems in the performance of your duties.

SUBJECT OF THE EXAMINATION:
The written test is designed to test for knowledge, skills, and/or abilities in such areas as:
1. **Supervision** - These questions test for knowledge of the principles and practices employed in planning, organizing, and controlling the activities of a work unit toward predetermined objectives. The concepts covered, usually in a situational question format, include such topics as assigning and reviewing work; evaluating performance; maintaining work standards; motivating and developing subordinates; implementing procedural change; increasing efficiency; and dealing with problems of absenteeism, morale, and discipline.
2. **Administrative supervision** - These questions test for knowledge of the principles and practices involved in directing the activities of a large subordinate staff, including subordinate supervisors. Questions relate to the personal interactions between an upper level supervisor and his/her subordinate supervisors in the accomplishment of objectives. These questions cover such areas as assigning work to and coordinating the activities of several units, establishing and guiding staff development programs, evaluating the performance of subordinate supervisors, and maintaining relationships with other organizational sections.
3. **Review and interpretation of plans and specifications, and the preparation of estimates** - These questions test for the ability to read and understand typical building plans, layouts, and technical specifications; and for the ability to calculate accurate estimates of material and labor costs.
4. **Work planning and scheduling** - These questions test for knowledge of the principles used in developing and implementing work plans and for the ability to arrange work assignments in a manner that will achieve work goals while staying within scheduling criteria. This may include setting up vacation or work schedules, taking into consideration such factors as seniority, work skills, duty hours, and shift coverage.

5. **Accident prevention and control** - These questions test for knowledge of the principles and practices of accident prevention and control and may cover such areas as causes of accidents, accident rates, behavior and attitudes of workers and supervisors, accident investigations and interviewing techniques, and types of accident prevention and safety programs.
6. **Maintenance management and energy conservation** - These questions test for knowledge of the principles and practices involved in managing a building maintenance and energy conservation program including such areas as determining the need for and scheduling building repairs; proper building maintenance techniques; and effective energy conservation practices for buildings, including optimal heating plant and cooling system operation.
7. **Operation, construction, alteration, and maintenance of physical plants, including mechanical and electrical equipment** - These questions test for knowledge of the methods and materials used in the construction, alteration, maintenance and repair of physical plant facilities including such areas as building foundation and framing, building hardware, insulation, and roofing; and building plumbing, electrical, sanitary, and heating, ventilating, and air conditioning systems.

HOW TO TAKE A TEST

I. YOU MUST PASS AN EXAMINATION

A. WHAT EVERY CANDIDATE SHOULD KNOW

Examination applicants often ask us for help in preparing for the written test. What can I study in advance? What kinds of questions will be asked? How will the test be given? How will the papers be graded?

As an applicant for a civil service examination, you may be wondering about some of these things. Our purpose here is to suggest effective methods of advance study and to describe civil service examinations.

Your chances for success on this examination can be increased if you know how to prepare. Those "pre-examination jitters" can be reduced if you know what to expect. You can even experience an adventure in good citizenship if you know why civil service exams are given.

B. WHY ARE CIVIL SERVICE EXAMINATIONS GIVEN?

Civil service examinations are important to you in two ways. As a citizen, you want public jobs filled by employees who know how to do their work. As a job seeker, you want a fair chance to compete for that job on an equal footing with other candidates. The best-known means of accomplishing this two-fold goal is the competitive examination.

Exams are widely publicized throughout the nation. They may be administered for jobs in federal, state, city, municipal, town or village governments or agencies.

Any citizen may apply, with some limitations, such as the age or residence of applicants. Your experience and education may be reviewed to see whether you meet the requirements for the particular examination. When these requirements exist, they are reasonable and applied consistently to all applicants. Thus, a competitive examination may cause you some uneasiness now, but it is your privilege and safeguard.

C. HOW ARE CIVIL SERVICE EXAMS DEVELOPED?

Examinations are carefully written by trained technicians who are specialists in the field known as "psychological measurement," in consultation with recognized authorities in the field of work that the test will cover. These experts recommend the subject matter areas or skills to be tested; only those knowledges or skills important to your success on the job are included. The most reliable books and source materials available are used as references. Together, the experts and technicians judge the difficulty level of the questions.

Test technicians know how to phrase questions so that the problem is clearly stated. Their ethics do not permit "trick" or "catch" questions. Questions may have been tried out on sample groups, or subjected to statistical analysis, to determine their usefulness.

Written tests are often used in combination with performance tests, ratings of training and experience, and oral interviews. All of these measures combine to form the best-known means of finding the right person for the right job.

II. HOW TO PASS THE WRITTEN TEST

A. NATURE OF THE EXAMINATION

To prepare intelligently for civil service examinations, you should know how they differ from school examinations you have taken. In school you were assigned certain definite pages to read or subjects to cover. The examination questions were quite detailed and usually emphasized memory. Civil service exams, on the other hand, try to discover your present ability to perform the duties of a position, plus your potentiality to learn these duties. In other words, a civil service exam attempts to predict how successful you will be. Questions cover such a broad area that they cannot be as minute and detailed as school exam questions.

In the public service similar kinds of work, or positions, are grouped together in one "class." This process is known as *position-classification*. All the positions in a class are paid according to the salary range for that class. One class title covers all of these positions, and they are all tested by the same examination.

B. FOUR BASIC STEPS

1) Study the announcement

How, then, can you know what subjects to study? Our best answer is: "Learn as much as possible about the class of positions for which you've applied." The exam will test the knowledge, skills and abilities needed to do the work.

Your most valuable source of information about the position you want is the official exam announcement. This announcement lists the training and experience qualifications. Check these standards and apply only if you come reasonably close to meeting them.

The brief description of the position in the examination announcement offers some clues to the subjects which will be tested. Think about the job itself. Review the duties in your mind. Can you perform them, or are there some in which you are rusty? Fill in the blank spots in your preparation.

Many jurisdictions preview the written test in the exam announcement by including a section called "Knowledge and Abilities Required," "Scope of the Examination," or some similar heading. Here you will find out specifically what fields will be tested.

2) Review your own background

Once you learn in general what the position is all about, and what you need to know to do the work, ask yourself which subjects you already know fairly well and which need improvement. You may wonder whether to concentrate on improving your strong areas or on building some background in your fields of weakness. When the announcement has specified "some knowledge" or "considerable knowledge," or has used adjectives like "beginning principles of..." or "advanced ... methods," you can get a clue as to the number and difficulty of questions to be asked in any given field. More questions, and hence broader coverage, would be included for those subjects which are more important in the work. Now weigh your strengths and weaknesses against the job requirements and prepare accordingly.

3) Determine the level of the position

Another way to tell how intensively you should prepare is to understand the level of the job for which you are applying. Is it the entering level? In other words, is this the position in which beginners in a field of work are hired? Or is it an intermediate or advanced level? Sometimes this is indicated by such words as "Junior" or "Senior" in the class title. Other jurisdictions use Roman numerals to designate the level – Clerk I, Clerk II, for example. The word "Supervisor" sometimes appears in the title. If the level is not indicated by the title, check the description of duties. Will you be working under very close supervision, or will you have responsibility for independent decisions in this work?

4) Choose appropriate study materials

Now that you know the subjects to be examined and the relative amount of each subject to be covered, you can choose suitable study materials. For beginning level jobs, or even advanced ones, if you have a pronounced weakness in some aspect of your training, read a modern, standard textbook in that field. Be sure it is up to date and has general coverage. Such books are normally available at your library, and the librarian will be glad to help you locate one. For entry-level positions, questions of appropriate difficulty are chosen – neither highly advanced questions, nor those too simple. Such questions require careful thought but not advanced training.

If the position for which you are applying is technical or advanced, you will read more advanced, specialized material. If you are already familiar with the basic principles of your field, elementary textbooks would waste your time. Concentrate on advanced textbooks and technical periodicals. Think through the concepts and review difficult problems in your field.

These are all general sources. You can get more ideas on your own initiative, following these leads. For example, training manuals and publications of the government agency which employs workers in your field can be useful, particularly for technical and professional positions. A letter or visit to the government department involved may result in more specific study suggestions, and certainly will provide you with a more definite idea of the exact nature of the position you are seeking.

III. KINDS OF TESTS

Tests are used for purposes other than measuring knowledge and ability to perform specified duties. For some positions, it is equally important to test ability to make adjustments to new situations or to profit from training. In others, basic mental abilities not dependent on information are essential. Questions which test these things may not appear as pertinent to the duties of the position as those which test for knowledge and information. Yet they are often highly important parts of a fair examination. For very general questions, it is almost impossible to help you direct your study efforts. What we can do is to point out some of the more common of these general abilities needed in public service positions and describe some typical questions.

1) General information

Broad, general information has been found useful for predicting job success in some kinds of work. This is tested in a variety of ways, from vocabulary lists to questions about current events. Basic background in some field of work, such as sociology or economics, may be sampled in a group of questions. Often these are principles which have become familiar to most persons through exposure rather than through formal training. It is difficult to advise you how to study for these questions; being alert to the world around you is our best suggestion.

2) Verbal ability

An example of an ability needed in many positions is verbal or language ability. Verbal ability is, in brief, the ability to use and understand words. Vocabulary and grammar tests are typical measures of this ability. Reading comprehension or paragraph interpretation questions are common in many kinds of civil service tests. You are given a paragraph of written material and asked to find its central meaning.

3) Numerical ability

Number skills can be tested by the familiar arithmetic problem, by checking paired lists of numbers to see which are alike and which are different, or by interpreting charts and graphs. In the latter test, a graph may be printed in the test booklet which you are asked to use as the basis for answering questions.

4) Observation

A popular test for law-enforcement positions is the observation test. A picture is shown to you for several minutes, then taken away. Questions about the picture test your ability to observe both details and larger elements.

5) Following directions

In many positions in the public service, the employee must be able to carry out written instructions dependably and accurately. You may be given a chart with several columns, each column listing a variety of information. The questions require you to carry out directions involving the information given in the chart.

6) Skills and aptitudes

Performance tests effectively measure some manual skills and aptitudes. When the skill is one in which you are trained, such as typing or shorthand, you can practice. These tests are often very much like those given in business school or high school courses. For many of the other skills and aptitudes, however, no short-time preparation can be made. Skills and abilities natural to you or that you have developed throughout your lifetime are being tested.

Many of the general questions just described provide all the data needed to answer the questions and ask you to use your reasoning ability to find the answers. Your best preparation for these tests, as well as for tests of facts and ideas, is to be at your physical and mental best. You, no doubt, have your own methods of getting into an exam-taking mood and keeping "in shape." The next section lists some ideas on this subject.

IV. KINDS OF QUESTIONS

Only rarely is the "essay" question, which you answer in narrative form, used in civil service tests. Civil service tests are usually of the short-answer type. Full instructions for answering these questions will be given to you at the examination. But in case this is your first experience with short-answer questions and separate answer sheets, here is what you need to know:

1) Multiple-choice Questions

Most popular of the short-answer questions is the "multiple choice" or "best answer" question. It can be used, for example, to test for factual knowledge, ability to solve problems or judgment in meeting situations found at work.

A multiple-choice question is normally one of three types—
- It can begin with an incomplete statement followed by several possible endings. You are to find the one ending which *best* completes the statement, although some of the others may not be entirely wrong.
- It can also be a complete statement in the form of a question which is answered by choosing one of the statements listed.

- It can be in the form of a problem – again you select the best answer.

Here is an example of a multiple-choice question with a discussion which should give you some clues as to the method for choosing the right answer:

When an employee has a complaint about his assignment, the action which will *best* help him overcome his difficulty is to
- A. discuss his difficulty with his coworkers
- B. take the problem to the head of the organization
- C. take the problem to the person who gave him the assignment
- D. say nothing to anyone about his complaint

In answering this question, you should study each of the choices to find which is best. Consider choice "A" – Certainly an employee may discuss his complaint with fellow employees, but no change or improvement can result, and the complaint remains unresolved. Choice "B" is a poor choice since the head of the organization probably does not know what assignment you have been given, and taking your problem to him is known as "going over the head" of the supervisor. The supervisor, or person who made the assignment, is the person who can clarify it or correct any injustice. Choice "C" is, therefore, correct. To say nothing, as in choice "D," is unwise. Supervisors have and interest in knowing the problems employees are facing, and the employee is seeking a solution to his problem.

2) True/False Questions

The "true/false" or "right/wrong" form of question is sometimes used. Here a complete statement is given. Your job is to decide whether the statement is right or wrong.

SAMPLE: A roaming cell-phone call to a nearby city costs less than a non-roaming call to a distant city.

This statement is wrong, or false, since roaming calls are more expensive.

This is not a complete list of all possible question forms, although most of the others are variations of these common types. You will always get complete directions for answering questions. Be sure you understand *how* to mark your answers – ask questions until you do.

V. RECORDING YOUR ANSWERS

Computer terminals are used more and more today for many different kinds of exams.

For an examination with very few applicants, you may be told to record your answers in the test booklet itself. Separate answer sheets are much more common. If this separate answer sheet is to be scored by machine – and this is often the case – it is highly important that you mark your answers correctly in order to get credit.

An electronic scoring machine is often used in civil service offices because of the speed with which papers can be scored. Machine-scored answer sheets must be marked with a pencil, which will be given to you. This pencil has a high graphite content which responds to the electronic scoring machine. As a matter of fact, stray dots may register as answers, so do not let your pencil rest on the answer sheet while you are pondering the correct answer. Also, if your pencil lead breaks or is otherwise defective, ask for another.

Since the answer sheet will be dropped in a slot in the scoring machine, be careful not to bend the corners or get the paper crumpled.

The answer sheet normally has five vertical columns of numbers, with 30 numbers to a column. These numbers correspond to the question numbers in your test booklet. After each number, going across the page are four or five pairs of dotted lines. These short dotted lines have small letters or numbers above them. The first two pairs may also have a "T" or "F" above the letters. This indicates that the first two pairs only are to be used if the questions are of the true-false type. If the questions are multiple choice, disregard the "T" and "F" and pay attention only to the small letters or numbers.

Answer your questions in the manner of the sample that follows:

32. The largest city in the United States is
    A. Washington, D.C.
    B. New York City
    C. Chicago
    D. Detroit
    E. San Francisco

1) Choose the answer you think is best. (New York City is the largest, so "B" is correct.)
2) Find the row of dotted lines numbered the same as the question you are answering. (Find row number 32)
3) Find the pair of dotted lines corresponding to the answer. (Find the pair of lines under the mark "B.")
4) Make a solid black mark between the dotted lines.

VI. BEFORE THE TEST

Common sense will help you find procedures to follow to get ready for an examination. Too many of us, however, overlook these sensible measures. Indeed, nervousness and fatigue have been found to be the most serious reasons why applicants fail to do their best on civil service tests. Here is a list of reminders:

- Begin your preparation early – Don't wait until the last minute to go scurrying around for books and materials or to find out what the position is all about.
- Prepare continuously – An hour a night for a week is better than an all-night cram session. This has been definitely established. What is more, a night a week for a month will return better dividends than crowding your study into a shorter period of time.
- Locate the place of the exam – You have been sent a notice telling you when and where to report for the examination. If the location is in a different town or otherwise unfamiliar to you, it would be well to inquire the best route and learn something about the building.
- Relax the night before the test – Allow your mind to rest. Do not study at all that night. Plan some mild recreation or diversion; then go to bed early and get a good night's sleep.
- Get up early enough to make a leisurely trip to the place for the test – This way unforeseen events, traffic snarls, unfamiliar buildings, etc. will not upset you.
- Dress comfortably – A written test is not a fashion show. You will be known by number and not by name, so wear something comfortable.

- Leave excess paraphernalia at home – Shopping bags and odd bundles will get in your way. You need bring only the items mentioned in the official notice you received; usually everything you need is provided. Do not bring reference books to the exam. They will only confuse those last minutes and be taken away from you when in the test room.
- Arrive somewhat ahead of time – If because of transportation schedules you must get there very early, bring a newspaper or magazine to take your mind off yourself while waiting.
- Locate the examination room – When you have found the proper room, you will be directed to the seat or part of the room where you will sit. Sometimes you are given a sheet of instructions to read while you are waiting. Do not fill out any forms until you are told to do so; just read them and be prepared.
- Relax and prepare to listen to the instructions
- If you have any physical problem that may keep you from doing your best, be sure to tell the test administrator. If you are sick or in poor health, you really cannot do your best on the exam. You can come back and take the test some other time.

VII. AT THE TEST

The day of the test is here and you have the test booklet in your hand. The temptation to get going is very strong. Caution! There is more to success than knowing the right answers. You must know how to identify your papers and understand variations in the type of short-answer question used in this particular examination. Follow these suggestions for maximum results from your efforts:

1) Cooperate with the monitor

The test administrator has a duty to create a situation in which you can be as much at ease as possible. He will give instructions, tell you when to begin, check to see that you are marking your answer sheet correctly, and so on. He is not there to guard you, although he will see that your competitors do not take unfair advantage. He wants to help you do your best.

2) Listen to all instructions

Don't jump the gun! Wait until you understand all directions. In most civil service tests you get more time than you need to answer the questions. So don't be in a hurry. Read each word of instructions until you clearly understand the meaning. Study the examples, listen to all announcements and follow directions. Ask questions if you do not understand what to do.

3) Identify your papers

Civil service exams are usually identified by number only. You will be assigned a number; you must not put your name on your test papers. Be sure to copy your number correctly. Since more than one exam may be given, copy your exact examination title.

4) Plan your time

Unless you are told that a test is a "speed" or "rate of work" test, speed itself is usually not important. Time enough to answer all the questions will be provided, but this does not mean that you have all day. An overall time limit has been set. Divide the total time (in minutes) by the number of questions to determine the approximate time you have for each question.

5) Do not linger over difficult questions

If you come across a difficult question, mark it with a paper clip (useful to have along) and come back to it when you have been through the booklet. One caution if you do this – be sure to skip a number on your answer sheet as well. Check often to be sure that you have not lost your place and that you are marking in the row numbered the same as the question you are answering.

6) Read the questions

Be sure you know what the question asks! Many capable people are unsuccessful because they failed to *read* the questions correctly.

7) Answer all questions

Unless you have been instructed that a penalty will be deducted for incorrect answers, it is better to guess than to omit a question.

8) Speed tests

It is often better NOT to guess on speed tests. It has been found that on timed tests people are tempted to spend the last few seconds before time is called in marking answers at random – without even reading them – in the hope of picking up a few extra points. To discourage this practice, the instructions may warn you that your score will be "corrected" for guessing. That is, a penalty will be applied. The incorrect answers will be deducted from the correct ones, or some other penalty formula will be used.

9) Review your answers

If you finish before time is called, go back to the questions you guessed or omitted to give them further thought. Review other answers if you have time.

10) Return your test materials

If you are ready to leave before others have finished or time is called, take ALL your materials to the monitor and leave quietly. Never take any test material with you. The monitor can discover whose papers are not complete, and taking a test booklet may be grounds for disqualification.

VIII. EXAMINATION TECHNIQUES

1) Read the general instructions carefully. These are usually printed on the first page of the exam booklet. As a rule, these instructions refer to the timing of the examination; the fact that you should not start work until the signal and must stop work at a signal, etc. If there are any *special* instructions, such as a choice of questions to be answered, make sure that you note this instruction carefully.

2) When you are ready to start work on the examination, that is as soon as the signal has been given, read the instructions to each question booklet, underline any key words or phrases, such as *least, best, outline, describe* and the like. In this way you will tend to answer as requested rather than discover on reviewing your paper that you *listed without describing*, that you selected the *worst* choice rather than the *best* choice, etc.

3) If the examination is of the objective or multiple-choice type – that is, each question will also give a series of possible answers: A, B, C or D, and you are called upon to select the best answer and write the letter next to that answer on your answer paper – it is advisable to start answering each question in turn. There may be anywhere from 50 to 100 such questions in the three or four hours allotted and you can see how much time would be taken if you read through all the questions before beginning to answer any. Furthermore, if you come across a question or group of questions which you know would be difficult to answer, it would undoubtedly affect your handling of all the other questions.

4) If the examination is of the essay type and contains but a few questions, it is a moot point as to whether you should read all the questions before starting to answer any one. Of course, if you are given a choice – say five out of seven and the like – then it is essential to read all the questions so you can eliminate the two that are most difficult. If, however, you are asked to answer all the questions, there may be danger in trying to answer the easiest one first because you may find that you will spend too much time on it. The best technique is to answer the first question, then proceed to the second, etc.

5) Time your answers. Before the exam begins, write down the time it started, then add the time allowed for the examination and write down the time it must be completed, then divide the time available somewhat as follows:
   - If 3-1/2 hours are allowed, that would be 210 minutes. If you have 80 objective-type questions, that would be an average of 2-1/2 minutes per question. Allow yourself no more than 2 minutes per question, or a total of 160 minutes, which will permit about 50 minutes to review.
   - If for the time allotment of 210 minutes there are 7 essay questions to answer, that would average about 30 minutes a question. Give yourself only 25 minutes per question so that you have about 35 minutes to review.

6) The most important instruction is to *read each question* and make sure you know what is wanted. The second most important instruction is to *time yourself properly* so that you answer every question. The third most important instruction is to *answer every question*. Guess if you have to but include something for each question. Remember that you will receive no credit for a blank and will probably receive some credit if you write something in answer to an essay question. If you guess a letter – say "B" for a multiple-choice question – you may have guessed right. If you leave a blank as an answer to a multiple-choice question, the examiners may respect your feelings but it will not add a point to your score. Some exams may penalize you for wrong answers, so in such cases *only*, you may not want to guess unless you have some basis for your answer.

7) Suggestions
   a. Objective-type questions
      1. Examine the question booklet for proper sequence of pages and questions
      2. Read all instructions carefully
      3. Skip any question which seems too difficult; return to it after all other questions have been answered
      4. Apportion your time properly; do not spend too much time on any single question or group of questions

5. Note and underline key words – *all, most, fewest, least, best, worst, same, opposite*, etc.
6. Pay particular attention to negatives
7. Note unusual option, e.g., unduly long, short, complex, different or similar in content to the body of the question
8. Observe the use of "hedging" words – *probably, may, most likely,* etc.
9. Make sure that your answer is put next to the same number as the question
10. Do not second-guess unless you have good reason to believe the second answer is definitely more correct
11. Cross out original answer if you decide another answer is more accurate; do not erase until you are ready to hand your paper in
12. Answer all questions; guess unless instructed otherwise
13. Leave time for review

b. Essay questions
  1. Read each question carefully
  2. Determine exactly what is wanted. Underline key words or phrases.
  3. Decide on outline or paragraph answer
  4. Include many different points and elements unless asked to develop any one or two points or elements
  5. Show impartiality by giving pros and cons unless directed to select one side only
  6. Make and write down any assumptions you find necessary to answer the questions
  7. Watch your English, grammar, punctuation and choice of words
  8. Time your answers; don't crowd material

8) Answering the essay question

Most essay questions can be answered by framing the specific response around several key words or ideas. Here are a few such key words or ideas:

M's: manpower, materials, methods, money, management
P's: purpose, program, policy, plan, procedure, practice, problems, pitfalls, personnel, public relations

  a. Six basic steps in handling problems:
    1. Preliminary plan and background development
    2. Collect information, data and facts
    3. Analyze and interpret information, data and facts
    4. Analyze and develop solutions as well as make recommendations
    5. Prepare report and sell recommendations
    6. Install recommendations and follow up effectiveness

  b. Pitfalls to avoid
    1. *Taking things for granted* – A statement of the situation does not necessarily imply that each of the elements is necessarily true; for example, a complaint may be invalid and biased so that all that can be taken for granted is that a complaint has been registered

2. *Considering only one side of a situation* – Wherever possible, indicate several alternatives and then point out the reasons you selected the best one
3. *Failing to indicate follow up* – Whenever your answer indicates action on your part, make certain that you will take proper follow-up action to see how successful your recommendations, procedures or actions turn out to be
4. *Taking too long in answering any single question* – Remember to time your answers properly

IX. AFTER THE TEST

Scoring procedures differ in detail among civil service jurisdictions although the general principles are the same. Whether the papers are hand-scored or graded by machine we have described, they are nearly always graded by number. That is, the person who marks the paper knows only the number – never the name – of the applicant. Not until all the papers have been graded will they be matched with names. If other tests, such as training and experience or oral interview ratings have been given, scores will be combined. Different parts of the examination usually have different weights. For example, the written test might count 60 percent of the final grade, and a rating of training and experience 40 percent. In many jurisdictions, veterans will have a certain number of points added to their grades.

After the final grade has been determined, the names are placed in grade order and an eligible list is established. There are various methods for resolving ties between those who get the same final grade – probably the most common is to place first the name of the person whose application was received first. Job offers are made from the eligible list in the order the names appear on it. You will be notified of your grade and your rank as soon as all these computations have been made. This will be done as rapidly as possible.

People who are found to meet the requirements in the announcement are called "eligibles." Their names are put on a list of eligible candidates. An eligible's chances of getting a job depend on how high he stands on this list and how fast agencies are filling jobs from the list.

When a job is to be filled from a list of eligibles, the agency asks for the names of people on the list of eligibles for that job. When the civil service commission receives this request, it sends to the agency the names of the three people highest on this list. Or, if the job to be filled has specialized requirements, the office sends the agency the names of the top three persons who meet these requirements from the general list.

The appointing officer makes a choice from among the three people whose names were sent to him. If the selected person accepts the appointment, the names of the others are put back on the list to be considered for future openings.

That is the rule in hiring from all kinds of eligible lists, whether they are for typist, carpenter, chemist, or something else. For every vacancy, the appointing officer has his choice of any one of the top three eligibles on the list. This explains why the person whose name is on top of the list sometimes does not get an appointment when some of the persons lower on the list do. If the appointing officer chooses the second or third eligible, the No. 1 eligible does not get a job at once, but stays on the list until he is appointed or the list is terminated.

X. HOW TO PASS THE INTERVIEW TEST

The examination for which you applied requires an oral interview test. You have already taken the written test and you are now being called for the interview test – the final part of the formal examination.

You may think that it is not possible to prepare for an interview test and that there are no procedures to follow during an interview. Our purpose is to point out some things you can do in advance that will help you and some good rules to follow and pitfalls to avoid while you are being interviewed.

What is an interview supposed to test?

The written examination is designed to test the technical knowledge and competence of the candidate; the oral is designed to evaluate intangible qualities, not readily measured otherwise, and to establish a list showing the relative fitness of each candidate – as measured against his competitors – for the position sought. Scoring is not on the basis of "right" and "wrong," but on a sliding scale of values ranging from "not passable" to "outstanding." As a matter of fact, it is possible to achieve a relatively low score without a single "incorrect" answer because of evident weakness in the qualities being measured.

Occasionally, an examination may consist entirely of an oral test – either an individual or a group oral. In such cases, information is sought concerning the technical knowledges and abilities of the candidate, since there has been no written examination for this purpose. More commonly, however, an oral test is used to supplement a written examination.

Who conducts interviews?

The composition of oral boards varies among different jurisdictions. In nearly all, a representative of the personnel department serves as chairman. One of the members of the board may be a representative of the department in which the candidate would work. In some cases, "outside experts" are used, and, frequently, a businessman or some other representative of the general public is asked to serve. Labor and management or other special groups may be represented. The aim is to secure the services of experts in the appropriate field.

However the board is composed, it is a good idea (and not at all improper or unethical) to ascertain in advance of the interview who the members are and what groups they represent. When you are introduced to them, you will have some idea of their backgrounds and interests, and at least you will not stutter and stammer over their names.

What should be done before the interview?

While knowledge about the board members is useful and takes some of the surprise element out of the interview, there is other preparation which is more substantive. It *is* possible to prepare for an oral interview – in several ways:

1) Keep a copy of your application and review it carefully before the interview

This may be the only document before the oral board, and the starting point of the interview. Know what education and experience you have listed there, and the sequence and dates of all of it. Sometimes the board will ask you to review the highlights of your experience for them; you should not have to hem and haw doing it.

2) Study the class specification and the examination announcement

Usually, the oral board has one or both of these to guide them. The qualities, characteristics or knowledges required by the position sought are stated in these documents. They offer valuable clues as to the nature of the oral interview. For example, if the job involves supervisory responsibilities, the announcement will usually indicate that knowledge of modern supervisory methods and the qualifications of the candidate as a supervisor will be tested. If so, you can expect such questions, frequently in the form of a hypothetical situation which you are expected to solve. NEVER go into an oral without knowledge of the duties and responsibilities of the job you seek.

3) Think through each qualification required

Try to visualize the kind of questions you would ask if you were a board member. How well could you answer them? Try especially to appraise your own knowledge and background in each area, *measured against the job sought*, and identify any areas in which you are weak. Be critical and realistic – do not flatter yourself.

4) Do some general reading in areas in which you feel you may be weak

For example, if the job involves supervision and your past experience has NOT, some general reading in supervisory methods and practices, particularly in the field of human relations, might be useful. Do NOT study agency procedures or detailed manuals. The oral board will be testing your understanding and capacity, not your memory.

5) Get a good night's sleep and watch your general health and mental attitude

You will want a clear head at the interview. Take care of a cold or any other minor ailment, and of course, no hangovers.

What should be done on the day of the interview?

Now comes the day of the interview itself. Give yourself plenty of time to get there. Plan to arrive somewhat ahead of the scheduled time, particularly if your appointment is in the fore part of the day. If a previous candidate fails to appear, the board might be ready for you a bit early. By early afternoon an oral board is almost invariably behind schedule if there are many candidates, and you may have to wait. Take along a book or magazine to read, or your application to review, but leave any extraneous material in the waiting room when you go in for your interview. In any event, relax and compose yourself.

The matter of dress is important. The board is forming impressions about you – from your experience, your manners, your attitude, and your appearance. Give your personal appearance careful attention. Dress your best, but not your flashiest. Choose conservative, appropriate clothing, and be sure it is immaculate. This is a business interview, and your appearance should indicate that you regard it as such. Besides, being well groomed and properly dressed will help boost your confidence.

Sooner or later, someone will call your name and escort you into the interview room. *This is it.* From here on you are on your own. It is too late for any more preparation. But remember, you asked for this opportunity to prove your fitness, and you are here because your request was granted.

What happens when you go in?

The usual sequence of events will be as follows: The clerk (who is often the board stenographer) will introduce you to the chairman of the oral board, who will introduce you to the other members of the board. Acknowledge the introductions before you sit down. Do not be surprised if you find a microphone facing you or a stenotypist sitting by. Oral interviews are usually recorded in the event of an appeal or other review.

Usually the chairman of the board will open the interview by reviewing the highlights of your education and work experience from your application – primarily for the benefit of the other members of the board, as well as to get the material into the record. Do not interrupt or comment unless there is an error or significant misinterpretation; if that is the case, do not hesitate. But do not quibble about insignificant matters. Also, he will usually ask you some question about your education, experience or your present job – partly to get you to start talking and to establish the interviewing "rapport." He may start the actual questioning, or turn it over to one of the other members. Frequently, each member undertakes the questioning on a particular area, one in which he is perhaps most competent, so you can expect each member to participate in the examination. Because time is limited, you may also expect some rather abrupt switches in the direction the questioning takes, so do not be upset by it. Normally, a board member will not pursue a single line of questioning unless he discovers a particular strength or weakness.

After each member has participated, the chairman will usually ask whether any member has any further questions, then will ask you if you have anything you wish to add. Unless you are expecting this question, it may floor you. Worse, it may start you off on an extended, extemporaneous speech. The board is not usually seeking more information. The question is principally to offer you a last opportunity to present further qualifications or to indicate that you have nothing to add. So, if you feel that a significant qualification or characteristic has been overlooked, it is proper to point it out in a sentence or so. Do not compliment the board on the thoroughness of their examination – they have been sketchy, and you know it. If you wish, merely say, "No thank you, I have nothing further to add." This is a point where you can "talk yourself out" of a good impression or fail to present an important bit of information. Remember, *you close the interview yourself.*

The chairman will then say, "That is all, Mr. _____, thank you." Do not be startled; the interview is over, and quicker than you think. Thank him, gather your belongings and take your leave. Save your sigh of relief for the other side of the door.

How to put your best foot forward

Throughout this entire process, you may feel that the board individually and collectively is trying to pierce your defenses, seek out your hidden weaknesses and embarrass and confuse you. Actually, this is not true. They are obliged to make an appraisal of your qualifications for the job you are seeking, and they want to see you in your best light. Remember, they must interview all candidates and a non-cooperative candidate may become a failure in spite of their best efforts to bring out his qualifications. Here are 15 suggestions that will help you:

1) Be natural – Keep your attitude confident, not cocky

If you are not confident that you can do the job, do not expect the board to be. Do not apologize for your weaknesses, try to bring out your strong points. The board is interested in a positive, not negative, presentation. Cockiness will antagonize any board member and make him wonder if you are covering up a weakness by a false show of strength.

2) Get comfortable, but don't lounge or sprawl

Sit erectly but not stiffly. A careless posture may lead the board to conclude that you are careless in other things, or at least that you are not impressed by the importance of the occasion. Either conclusion is natural, even if incorrect. Do not fuss with your clothing, a pencil or an ashtray. Your hands may occasionally be useful to emphasize a point; do not let them become a point of distraction.

3) Do not wisecrack or make small talk

This is a serious situation, and your attitude should show that you consider it as such. Further, the time of the board is limited – they do not want to waste it, and neither should you.

4) Do not exaggerate your experience or abilities

In the first place, from information in the application or other interviews and sources, the board may know more about you than you think. Secondly, you probably will not get away with it. An experienced board is rather adept at spotting such a situation, so do not take the chance.

5) If you know a board member, do not make a point of it, yet do not hide it

Certainly you are not fooling him, and probably not the other members of the board. Do not try to take advantage of your acquaintanceship – it will probably do you little good.

6) Do not dominate the interview

Let the board do that. They will give you the clues – do not assume that you have to do all the talking. Realize that the board has a number of questions to ask you, and do not try to take up all the interview time by showing off your extensive knowledge of the answer to the first one.

7) Be attentive

You only have 20 minutes or so, and you should keep your attention at its sharpest throughout. When a member is addressing a problem or question to you, give him your undivided attention. Address your reply principally to him, but do not exclude the other board members.

8) Do not interrupt

A board member may be stating a problem for you to analyze. He will ask you a question when the time comes. Let him state the problem, and wait for the question.

9) Make sure you understand the question

Do not try to answer until you are sure what the question is. If it is not clear, restate it in your own words or ask the board member to clarify it for you. However, do not haggle about minor elements.

10) Reply promptly but not hastily

A common entry on oral board rating sheets is "candidate responded readily," or "candidate hesitated in replies." Respond as promptly and quickly as you can, but do not jump to a hasty, ill-considered answer.

11) Do not be peremptory in your answers

A brief answer is proper – but do not fire your answer back. That is a losing game from your point of view. The board member can probably ask questions much faster than you can answer them.

12) Do not try to create the answer you think the board member wants

He is interested in what kind of mind you have and how it works – not in playing games. Furthermore, he can usually spot this practice and will actually grade you down on it.

13) Do not switch sides in your reply merely to agree with a board member

Frequently, a member will take a contrary position merely to draw you out and to see if you are willing and able to defend your point of view. Do not start a debate, yet do not surrender a good position. If a position is worth taking, it is worth defending.

14) Do not be afraid to admit an error in judgment if you are shown to be wrong

The board knows that you are forced to reply without any opportunity for careful consideration. Your answer may be demonstrably wrong. If so, admit it and get on with the interview.

15) Do not dwell at length on your present job

The opening question may relate to your present assignment. Answer the question but do not go into an extended discussion. You are being examined for a *new* job, not your present one. As a matter of fact, try to phrase ALL your answers in terms of the job for which you are being examined.

Basis of Rating

Probably you will forget most of these "do's" and "don'ts" when you walk into the oral interview room. Even remembering them all will not ensure you a passing grade. Perhaps you did not have the qualifications in the first place. But remembering them will help you to put your best foot forward, without treading on the toes of the board members.

Rumor and popular opinion to the contrary notwithstanding, an oral board wants you to make the best appearance possible. They know you are under pressure – but they also want to see how you respond to it as a guide to what your reaction would be under the pressures of the job you seek. They will be influenced by the degree of poise you display, the personal traits you show and the manner in which you respond.

ABOUT THIS BOOK

This book contains tests divided into Examination Sections. Go through each test, answering every question in the margin. We have also attached a sample answer sheet at the back of the book that can be removed and used. At the end of each test look at the answer key and check your answers. On the ones you got wrong, look at the right answer choice and learn. Do not fill in the answers first. Do not memorize the questions and answers, but understand the answer and principles involved. On your test, the questions will likely be different from the samples. Questions are changed and new ones added. If you understand these past questions you should have success with any changes that arise. Tests may consist of several types of questions. We have additional books on each subject should more study be advisable or necessary for you. Finally, the more you study, the better prepared you will be. This book is intended to be the last thing you study before you walk into the examination room. Prior study of relevant texts is also recommended. NLC publishes some of these in our Fundamental Series. Knowledge and good sense are important factors in passing your exam. Good luck also helps. So now study this Passbook, absorb the material contained within and take that knowledge into the examination. Then do your best to pass that exam.

EXAMINATION SECTION

EXAMINATION SECTION
TEST 1

DIRECTIONS: Each question or incomplete statement is followed by several suggested answers or completions. Select the one that BEST answers the question or completes the statement. *PRINT THE LETTER OF THE CORRECT ANSWER IN THE SPACE AT THE RIGHT.*

1.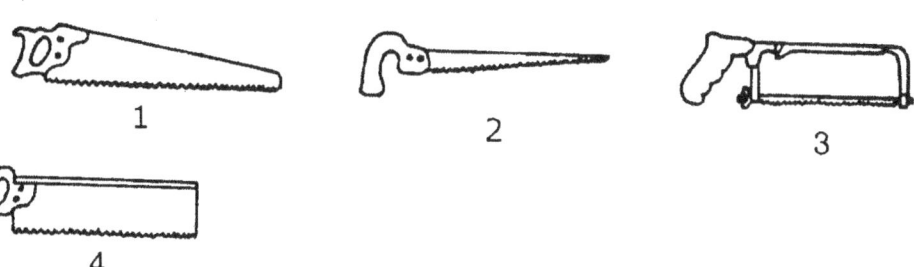

   The saw that is used PRINCIPALLY where curved cuts are to be made is numbered

   A. 1   B. 2   C. 3   D. 4

2.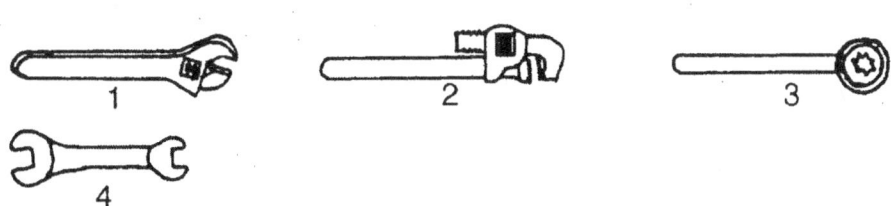

   The wrench that is used PRINCIPALLY for pipe work is numbered

   A. 1   B. 2   C. 3   D. 4

3.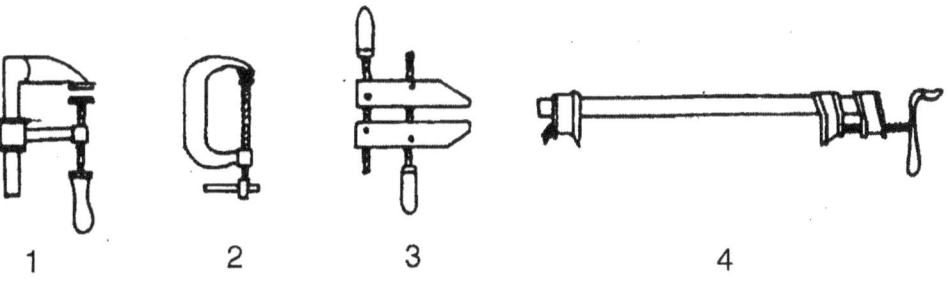

   The carpenter's *hand screw* is numbered

   A. 1   B. 2   C. 3   D. 4

1

4.

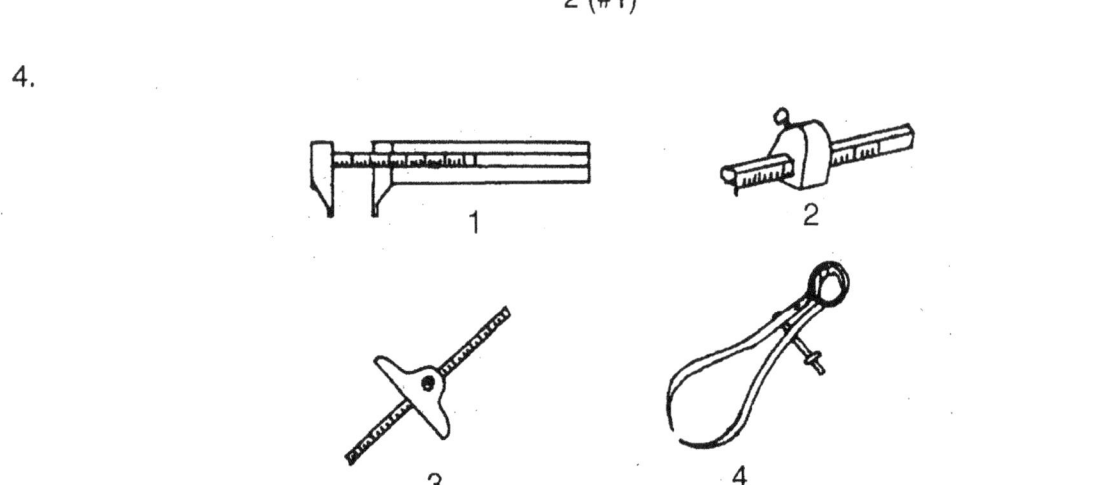

The tool used to measure the depth of a hole is numbered

   A. 1   B. 2   C. 3   D. 4

5.

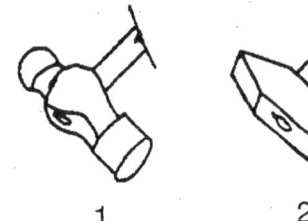  

The tool that is BEST suited for use with a wood chisel is numbered

   A. 1   B. 2   C. 3   D. 4

6.

The screw head that would be tightened with an *Allen* wrench is numbered

   A. 1   B. 2   C. 3   D. 4

7.

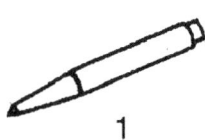 

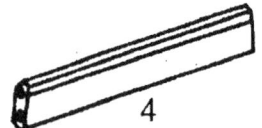

The center punch is numbered

   A. 1   B. 2   C. 3   D. 4

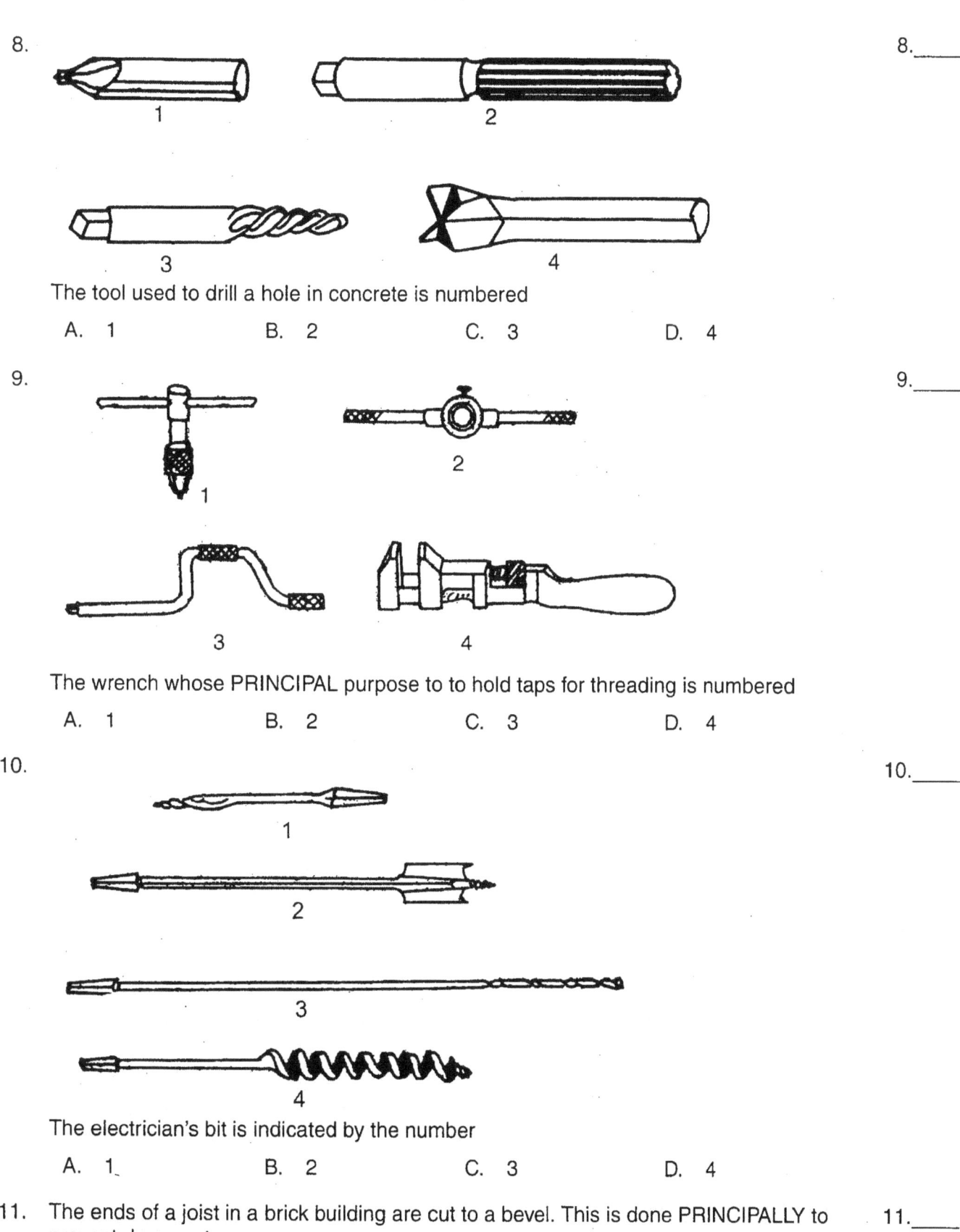

8. The tool used to drill a hole in concrete is numbered

   A. 1 B. 2 C. 3 D. 4

9. The wrench whose PRINCIPAL purpose to to hold taps for threading is numbered

   A. 1 B. 2 C. 3 D. 4

10. The electrician's bit is indicated by the number

    A. 1 B. 2 C. 3 D. 4

11. The ends of a joist in a brick building are cut to a bevel. This is done PRINCIPALLY to prevent damage to

    A. joist B. floor C. sill D. wall

12. Of the following, the wood that is MOST commonly used today for floor joists is 12.___

    A. long leaf yellow pine B. douglas fir
    C. oak D. birch

13. Quarter-sawed lumber is preferred for the BEST finished flooring PRINCIPALLY because it 13.___

    A. has the greatest strength B. shrinks the least
    C. is the easiest to nail D. is the easiest to handle

14. A tool used in hanging doors is a 14.___

    A. miter gauge B. line level
    C. try square D. butt gauge

15. Of the following, the MAXIMUM height that would be considered acceptable for a stair riser is 15.___

    A. 6 1/2" B. 7 1/2" C. 8 1/2" D. 9 1/2"

16. The PRINCIPAL reason for *cross banding* the layers of wood in a plywood panel is to _____ of the panel. 16.___

    A. reduce warping B. increase the strength
    C. reduce the cost D. increase the beauty

17. The part of a tree that will produce the DENSEST wood is the _____ wood. 17.___

    A. spring B. summer C. sap D. heart

18. Casing nails MOST NEARLY resemble _____ nails. 18.___

    A. common B. roofing C. form D. finishing

19. Lumber in quantity is ordered by 19.___

    A. cubic feet B. foot board measure
    C. lineal feet D. weight and length

20. For finishing of wood, BEST results are obtained by sanding 20.___

    A. with a circular motion
    B. against the grain
    C. with the grain
    D. with a circular motion on edges and against the grain on the flat parts

21. A *chase* in a brick wall is a 21.___

    A. pilaster B. waterstop C. recess D. corbel

22. Parging refers to 22.___

    A. increasing the thickness of a brick wall
    B. plastering the back of face brickwork
    C. bonding face brick to backing blocks
    D. leveling each course of brick

23. The PRINCIPAL reason for requiring brick to be wetted before laying is that

    A. less water is required in the mortar
    B. efflorescence is prevented
    C. the brick will not absorb as much water from the mortar
    D. cool brick is easier to handle

24. In brickwork, muriatic acid is commonly used to

    A. increase the strength of the mortar
    B. etch the brick
    C. waterproof the wall
    D. clean the wall

25. Cement mortar can be made easier to work by the addition of a small quantity of

    A. lime B. soda C. litharge D. plaster

26. Headers in brickwork are used to _____ the wall.

    A. strengthen
    B. reduce the cost of
    C. speed the erection of
    D. align

27. Joints in brick walls are tooled

    A. immediately after each brick is laid
    B. after the mortar has had its initial set
    C. after the entire wall is completed
    D. 28 days after the wall has been built

28. If cement mortar has begun to set before it can be used in a wall, the BEST thing to do is to

    A. use the mortar immediately as is
    B. add a small quantity of lime
    C. add some water and mix thoroughly
    D. discard the mortar

29. A *bat* in brickwork is a

    A. brace to hold a wall temporarily in place
    B. stick used to aid in mixing of mortar
    C. broken piece of brick used to fill short spaces
    D. curved brick used in ornamental work

30. The proportions by volume of cement, lime, and sand in a cement-lime mortar should be, according to the Building Code,

    A. 1:1:3 B. 2:1:6 C. 1:1:6 D. 1:2:6

31. The BEST flux to use when soldering galvanized iron is

    A. killed acid
    B. sal-ammoniac
    C. muriatic acid
    D. resin

32. When soldering a vertical joint, the soldering iron should be tinned on _____ side(s).
    A. 1   B. 2   C. 3   D. 4

33. The difference between *right hand* and *left hand* tin snips is the
    A. relative position of the cutting jaws
    B. shape of the cutting jaws
    C. shape of the handles
    D. relative position of the handles

34. A machine used to bend sheet metal is called a
    A. router   B. planer   C. brake   D. swage

35. The type of solder that would be used in *hard soldering* would be _____ solder.
    A. bismuth   B. wiping   C. 50-50   D. silver

36. Roll roofing material is usually felt which has been impregnated with
    A. cement   B. mastic   C. tar   D. latex

37. The purpose of flashing on roofs is to
    A. secure roofing materials to the roof
    B. make it easier to lay the roofing
    C. prevent leaks through the roof
    D. insulate the roof from excessive heat

38. The tool used to spread hot pitch on a three-ply roofing job is a
    A. mop   B. spreader   C. pusher   D. broom

39. The cutting of glass can be facilitated by dipping the cutting wheel in
    A. *3-in-1* oil   B. water   C. lard   D. kerosene

40. The strips of metal used to hold glass to the window frame while it is being puttied are called
    A. hold-downs   B. points   C. wedges   D. triangles

41. The type of chain used with sash weights is _____ link.
    A. flat
    B. round
    C. figure-eight
    D. basket-weave

42. The material that would be used to seal around a window frame is
    A. oakum   B. litharge   C. grout   D. calking

43. The function of a window sill is MOST NEARLY the same as that of a
    A. jamb   B. coping   C. lintel   D. brick

44. Lightweight plaster would be made with
    A. sand   B. cinders   C. potash   D. vermiculite

45. The FIRST coat of plaster to be applied on a three-coat plaster job is the _____ coat.   45.____

    A. brown   B. scratch   C. white   D. keene

46. Screeds in plaster work are used to   46.____

    A. remove larger sizes of sand
    B. hold the batch of plaster before it is applied
    C. apply the plaster to the wall
    D. guide the plasterer in making, an even wall

47. The FIRST coat of plaster over rock lath should be a _____ plaster.   47.____

    A. gypsum   B. lime
    C. portland cement   D. puzzolan cement

48. In plastering, a *hawk* is used to _____ plaster.   48.____

    A. apply   B. hold   C. scratch   D. smooth

49. When mixing concrete by hand, the order in which the ingredients should be mixed is: 49.____

    A. water, cement, sand, stone
    B. sand, cement, water, stone
    C. stone, water, sand, cement
    D. stone, sand, cement, water

50. The PRINCIPAL reason for covering a concrete sidewalk with straw or paper after the concrete has been poured is to   50.____

    A. prevent people from walking on the concrete while it is still wet
    B. impart a rough non-slip surface to the concrete
    C. prevent excessive evaporation of water in the concrete
    D. shorten the length of time it would take for the concrete to harden

---

KEY (CORRECT ANSWERS)

1. B	11. D	21. C	31. C	41. A
2. B	12. B	22. B	32. A	42. D
3. C	13. B	23. C	33. A	43. B
4. C	14. D	24. D	34. C	44. D
5. D	15. B	25. A	35. D	45. B
6. C	16. A	26. A	36. C	46. D
7. A	17. D	27. B	37. C	47. A
8. D	18. D	28. D	38. A	48. B
9. A	19. B	29. C	39. D	49. D
10. C	20. C	30. C	40. B	50. C

TEST 2

DIRECTIONS: Each question or incomplete statement is followed by several suggested answers or completions. Select the one that BEST answers the question or completes the statement. *PRINT THE LETTER OF THE CORRECT ANSWER IN THE SPACE AT THE RIGHT.*

1. When colored concrete is required, the colors used should be

    A. colors in oil
    B. mineral pigments
    C. tempera colors
    D. water colors

    1.____

2. Concrete is *rubbed* with a(n)

    A. emery wheel
    B. carborundum brick
    C. sandstone
    D. alundum stick

    2.____

3. To prevent concrete from sticking to forms, the forms should be painted with

    A. oil   B. kerosene   C. water   D. lime

    3.____

4. The reinforcement in a concrete floor slab is referred to as 6"-6" x #6-#6. The type of reinforcing that is being used is

    A. steel bars
    B. wire mesh
    C. angle irons
    D. grating plate

    4.____

5. One method of measuring the consistency of a concrete mix is by means of a _____ test.

    A. penetration   B. flow   C. slump   D. weight

    5.____

6. A chemical that is sometimes used to prevent the freezing of concrete in cold weather is

    A. alum
    B. glycerine
    C. calcium chloride
    D. sodium nitrate

    6.____

7. The one of the following that is LEAST commonly used for columns is

    A. wide flange beams
    B. angles
    C. concrete-filled pipe
    D. *I* beams

    7.____

8. Fire protection of steel floor beams is MOST frequently accomplished by the use of

    A. gypsum block
    B. brick
    C. rock wool fill
    D. vermiculite gypsum plaster

    8.____

9. A *Pittsburgh lock* is a(n)

    A. emergency door lock
    B. sheet metal joint
    C. elevator safety
    D. boiler valve

    9.____

10. In order to drill a hole at right angle to the horizontal axis of a round bar, the bar should be held in a

    A. step block
    B. C-block
    C. hand pliers
    D. V-block

    10.____

11. The procedure to follow in the lubrication of maintenance shop equipment is to lubricate   11.____

    A. when you can spare the time
    B. only when necessary
    C. at regular intervals
    D. when the equipment is in operation

12. Of the following items, the one which is NOT used in making fastenings to masonry or plaster walls is a(n)   12.____

    A. lead shield   B. expansion bolt
    C. rawl plug   D. steel bushing

13. When a common straight ladder is used to paint a wall, the safe distance that the foot of the ladder should be set away from the wall is MOST NEARLY _____ the length of the ladder.   13.____

    A. one-eighth   B. one-quarter
    C. one-half   D. five-eighths

14. The term *bell and spigot* usually refers to   14.____

    A. refrigerator motors   B. cast iron pipes
    C. steam radiator outlets D. electrical receptacles

15. In plumbing work, a valve which allows water to flow in one direction only is commonly known as a _____ valve.   15.____

    A. check   B. globe   C. gate   D. stop

16. A pipe coupling is BEST used to connect two pieces of pipe of   16.____

    A. the same diameter in a straight line
    B. the same diameter at right angles to each other
    C. different diameters at a 45° angle
    D. different diameters at an 1/8th bend

17. A fitting or pipe with many outlets relatively close together is commonly called a   17.____

    A. manifold   B. gooseneck
    C. flange union   D. return bend

18. To locate the center in the end of a sound shaft, the BEST tool to use is a(n)   18.____

    A. ruler   B. divider
    C. hermaphrodite caliper   D. micrometer

19. When cutting a piece of 1 1/4" O.D. 20 gauge brass tubing with a hand hacksaw, it is BEST to use a blade having _____ teeth per inch.   19.____

    A. 14   B. 18   C. 22   D. 32

20. When cutting a piece of 1" O.D. extra-heavy pipe with a pipe cutter, a burr usually forms on the inside and the outside of the pipe. These burrs are BEST removed by means of a pipe   20.____

    A. tap and a file   B. wrench and rough stone
    C. reamer and a file   D. drill and a chisel

21. Artificial respiration should be started immediately on a man who has suffered an electric shock if he is

    A. *unconscious* and breathing
    B. *unconscious* and not breathing
    C. *conscious* and in a daze
    D. *conscious* and badly burned

22. The fuse of a certain circuit has blown and is replaced with a fuse of the same rating which also blows when the switch is closed.
    In this case,

    A. a fuse of higher current rating should be used
    B. a fuse of higher voltage rating should be used
    C. the fuse should be temporarily replaced by a heavy piece of wire
    D. the circuit should be checked

23. Operating an incandescent electric light bulb at less than its rated voltage will result in

    A. shorter life and brighter light
    B. longer life and dimmer light
    C. brighter light and longer life
    D. dimmer light and shorter life

24. In order to control a lamp from two different positions, it is necessary to use

    A. two single pole switches
    B. one single pole switch and one four-way switch
    C. two three-way switches
    D. one single pole switch and one four-way switch

25.

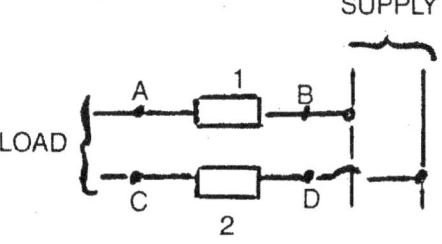

    One method of testing fuses is to connect a pair of test lamps in the circuit in such a manner that the test lamp will light up if the fuse is good and will remain dark if the fuse is bad. In the above illustration 1 and 2 are fuses.
    In order to test if fuse 1 is bad, test lamps should be connected between

    A. A and B   B. B and D   C. A and D   D. C and B

26. The PRINCIPAL reason for the grounding of electrical equipment and circuits is to

    A. prevent short circuits   B. insure safety from shock
    C. save power   D. increase voltage

27. The ordinary single-pole flush wall type switch must be connected   27._____

    A. across the line   B. in the *hot* conductor
    C. in the grounded conductor   D. in the white conductor

28. A D.C. shunt motor runs in the wrong direction. This fault can be CORRECTED by   28._____

    A. reversing the connections of both the field and the armature
    B. interchanging the connections of either main or auxiliar windings
    C. interchanging the connections to either the field or the armature windings
    D. interchanging the connections to the line of the power leads

29. The MOST common type of motor that can be used with both A.C. and D.C. sources is the _____ motor.   29._____

    A. compound   B. repulsion   C. series   D. shunt

30. A fluorescent fixture in a new building has been in use for several months without trouble. Recently, the ends of the fluorscent lamp have remained lighted when the light was switched off.
The BEST way to clear up this trouble is to replace the   30._____

    A. lamp   B. ballast   C. starter   D. sockets

31. The BEST wood to use for handles of tools such as axes and hammers is   31._____

    A. hemlock   B. pine   C. oak   D. hickory

32. A *hanger bolt*   32._____

    A. has a square head
    B. is bent in a *U* shape
    C. has a different type of thread at each end
    D. is threaded the entire length from point to head

33. A stone frequently used to sharpen tools is   33._____

    A. carborundum   B. bauxite   C. resin   D. slate

34. A strike plate is MOST closely associated with a   34._____

    A. lock   B. sash   C. butt   D. tie rod

35. The material that distinguishes a terrazzo floor from an ordinary concrete floor is   35._____

    A. cinders   B. marble chip
    C. cut stone   D. non-slip aggregate

36. A room is 7'6" wide by 9'0" long with a ceiling height of 8'0". One gallon of flat paint will cover approximately 400 square feet of wall.
The number of gallons of this paint required to paint the walls of this room, making no deductions for windows or doors, is MOST NEARLY _____ gallon.   36._____

    A. 1/4   B. 1/2   C. 3/4   D. 1

37. The cost of a certain job is broken down as follows:
    Materials $375
    Rental of equipment 120
    Labor   315
    The percentage of the total cost of the job that can be charged to materials is MOST NEARLY

    A. 40%   B. 42%   C. 44%   D. 46%

38. By trial, it is found that by using two cubic feet of sand, a five cubic foot batch of concrete is produced.
    Using the same proportions, the amount of sand required to produce 2 cubic yards of concrete is MOST NEARLY _____ cu.ft.

    A. 20   B. 22   C. 24   D. 26

39. It takes 4 men 6 days to do a certain job.
    Working at the same speed, the number of days it will take 3 men to do this job is

    A. 7   B. 8   C. 9   D. 10

40. The cost of rawl plugs is $2.75 per gross. The cost of 2,448 rawl plugs is

    A. $46.75   B. $47.25   C. $47.75   D. $48.25

41. *Rigidity* of the hammer handle enables the operator to control and direct the force of the blow.
    As used above, *rigidity* means MOST NEARLY

    A. straightness   B. strength
    C. shape   D. stiffness

42. *For precision work, center punches are ground to a fine tapered point.* As used above, *tapered* means MOST NEARLY

    A. conical   B. straight   C. accurate   D. smooth

43. *There are limitations to the drilling of metals by hand power.*
    As used above, *limitations* means MOST NEARLY

    A. advantages   B. restrictions
    C. difficulties   D. benefits

Questions 44-45.

DIRECTIONS: Questions 44 and 45 are based on the following paragraph.

Because electric drills run at high speed, the cutting edges of a twist drill are heated quickly. If the metal is thick, the drill point must be withdrawn from the hole frequently to cool it and clear out chips. Forcing the drill continuously into a deep hole will heat it, thereby spoiling its temper and cutting edges. A portable electric drill has the advantage that it can be taken to the work and used to drill holes in material too large to handle in a drill press.

44. According to the above paragraph, overheating of a twist drill will

    A. slow down the work   B. cause excessive drill breakage
    C. dull the drill   D. spoil the accuracy of the work

45. According to the above paragraph, one method of preventing overheating of a twist drill is to 45._____

    A. use cooling oil
    B. drill a smaller pilot hole first
    C. use a drill press
    D. remove the drill from the work frequently

Questions 46-50.

DIRECTIONS: Questions 46 to 50 are to be answered in accordance with the sketch shown below.

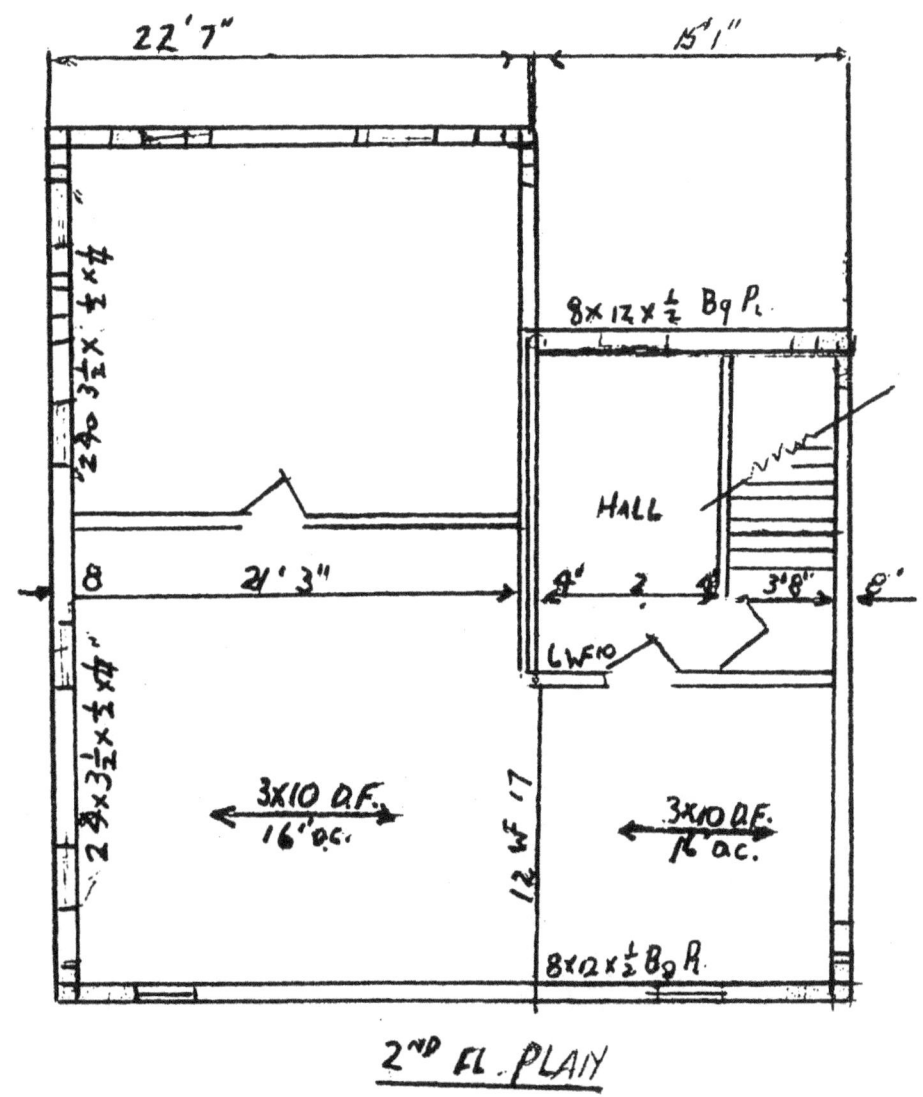

46. The one of the following statements that is CORRECT is the building 46._____

    A. is of fireproof construction
    B. has masonry walls with wood joists
    C. is of wood frame construction
    D. has timber joists and girders

47. The one of the following statements that is CORRECT is 47.___

    A. the stairway from the ground continues through the roof
    B. there are two means of egress from the second floor of this building
    C. the door on the second floor stair landing opens in the direction of egress
    D. the entire stair is shown on this plan

48. The width of the hall is 48.___

    A. 10'3" B. 10'5" C. 10'7" D. 10'9"

49. The lintels shown are 49.___

    A. angles
    C. an I-beam
    B. a channel and an angle
    D. precast concrete

50. The one of the following statements that is CORRECT is that the steel beam is 50.___

    A. supported by columns at the center and at the ends
    B. entirely supported by the walls
    C. supported on columns at the ends only
    D. supported at the center by a column and at the ends by the walls

---

KEY (CORRECT ANSWERS)

1. B	11. C	21. B	31. D	41. D
2. B	12. D	22. D	32. C	42. A
3. A	13. B	23. B	33. A	43. B
4. B	14. B	24. C	34. A	44. C
5. C	15. A	25. C	35. B	45. D
6. C	16. A	26. B	36. C	46. B
7. B	17. A	27. B	37. D	47. C
8. D	18. C	28. C	38. B	48. D
9. B	19. D	29. C	39. B	49. A
10. D	20. C	30. C	40. A	50. D

EXAMINATION SECTION
TEST 1

DIRECTIONS: Each question or incomplete statement is followed by several suggested answers or completions. Select the one that BEST answers the question or completes the statement. *PRINT THE LETTER OF THE CORRECT ANSWER IN THE SPACE AT THE RIGHT.*

1. A maintenance man complains to you that he is getting all the boring jobs to do. You check and find that his complaint has no basis in fact.
   The one of the following which is the MOST likely reason why the maintenance man made such a claim is that he

   A. wants to get even with the supervisor
   B. lives in a world of fantasy
   C. believes the injustice to be real
   D. is jealous of other workers

2. When on preliminary review of a mechanic's written grievance you feel the grievance to be unfounded, the FIRST step you should take is to

   A. show the mechanic where he is wrong
   B. check carefully to find out why the mechanic thinks that way
   C. try to humor the mechanic out of it
   D. tell the mechanic to stop complaining

3. Assume that you decide to hold a private meeting with one of your mechanics who has a drinking problem that is affecting his work.
   At the meeting, the BEST way for you to handle this situation is to

   A. tell the mechanic off and then listen to what he has to say
   B. criticize the mechanic's behavior to get him to *open up* in order to help him correct his problem quickly
   C. try to get the mechanic to recognize his problem and find ways to solve it
   D. limit the discussion to matters concerning only the problem and look for immediate results

4. The one of the following which is a generally accepted guide in criticizing a subordinate EFFECTIVELY is to

   A. criticize the improper act, not the individual
   B. put the listener on the defensive
   C. make the criticism general instead of specific
   D. correct the personality, not the situation

5. The one of the following disciplinary methods by which you are MOST likely to be successful in getting a problem employee to improve his behavior is when you

   A. discipline the employee in front of others
   B. consider the matter to be ended after the disciplining
   C. give the exact same discipline no matter how serious the wrongdoing
   D. make an example of the employee

6. Of the following statements, the one that is MOST applicable to a disciplinary situation is that discipline should be

   A. used after a cooling-off period
   B. identical for all employees
   C. consistent with the violation
   D. based on personal feelings

7. The one of the following approaches that is MOST important for you to take in evaluating a mechanic in order to increase his work productivity is to

   A. first have him evaluate his own performance
   B. meet with him to discuss how he is doing and what is expected on the job
   C. send him a copy of your evaluation of his work performance and give him the opportunity to submit written comments
   D. express in writing your appreciation of his work

8. Assume that you say to one of the mechanics, *Jim, that job you turned out today was top-notch. I didn't think you could do so well with the kind of material you had to work with.*
   This statement BEST describes an example of your

   A. recognition of the man's work
   B. disrespect for the man's feelings
   C. personal favoritism of the man
   D. constructive criticism of the man's work

9. In general, the OUTSTANDING characteristic of employees over 50 years of age is their

   A. resistance   B. endurance
   C. wisdom   D. job stability

10. You should be interested in the morale of your men because morale is MOST often associated with

    A. mechanization   B. automation
    C. production   D. seniority regulations

11. Assume that the maintenance work order system is about to be changed. Your workers would MOST likely show the LEAST resistance to this change if you

    A. downgrade the old maintenance work order system
    B. tell your workers how the change will benefit them
    C. post the notice of the change on the bulletin board
    D. tell the workers how the change will benefit management

12. Of the following, the BEST way to motivate a newly appointed mechanic is to

    A. explain the meaning of each assignment
    B. make the work more physically demanding
    C. test the mechanic's ability
    D. use as much authority as possible

13. The one of the following which is the LEAST important reason for giving employees information concerning policy changes which will affect them is that employees should know

    A. why the change is being made
    B. who will be affected by the change
    C. when the change will go into effect
    D. how much savings will be made by the change

14. A foreman who knows how to handle his men will MOST likely get them to produce more by treating them

    A. alike
    B. as individuals
    C. on a casual basis
    D. as a group

15. Of the following items, the one that a supervisor has the MOST right to expect from his employees is

    A. liking the job
    B. a fair day's work
    C. equal skill of all mechanics
    D. perfection

16. The one of the following which is the BEST practice for you to follow in handling a dispute between the workers is to

    A. side with one of the workers so as to end the dispute quickly
    B. pay no attention to the dispute and let the workers settle it themselves
    C. listen to each worker's story of the dispute and then decide how to settle it
    D. discuss the dispute with other workers and then decide how to settle it

17. You are likely to run into an employee morale problem when assigning a dirty job that comes up often.
    Of the following, the BEST method of assigning this work is to

    A. rotate this assignment
    B. assign it to the fastest worker
    C. assign it by seniority
    D. assign it to the least skilled worker

18. Of the following, the one that is generally regarded as the BEST aid to high work productivity of subordinates is a supervisor's skill in

    A. record keeping
    B. technical work
    C. setting up rules and regulations
    D. human relations

19. The BEST way to help a mechanic who comes to you for advice on a personal problem is to

    A. listen to the worker's problem without passing judgment
    B. tell the worker to forget about the problem and to stop letting it interfere with his work
    C. talk about your own personal problems to the worker
    D. mind your own business and leave the worker alone

20. You are in charge of the maintenance shop and have learned that within the next two weeks the maintenance shop will be moved to a new location on the plant grounds, but you have not learned why this move is taking place. Assume that you have decided not to keep this information from your mechanics until the reason is known but to inform them of this matter now.
Of the following, which one is the BEST argument that can be made regarding your decision?

    A. *Acceptable;* because although the reason is not now known, the mechanics will eventually find out about the move
    B. *Unacceptable;* because the mechanics do not know at this time the reason for the move and this will cause anxiety on their part
    C. *Acceptable*; because the mechanics will be affected by the move and they should be told what is happening
    D. *Unacceptable;* because the mechanics' advance knowledge of the move will tend to slow down their work output

21. Of the following, the FIRST action for a foreman to take in making a decision is to

    A. get all the facts
    B. develop alternate solutions
    C. get opinions of others
    D. know the results in advance

22. Assume that you have just been promoted to foreman.
Of the following, the BEST practice to follow regarding your previous experience at the mechanic's level is to

    A. continue to fraternize with your old friends
    B. use this experience to better understand those who now work for you
    C. use your old connections to keep top management informed of mechanics' views
    D. forget the mechanics' points of view

23. You have decided to hold regular group discussions with your subordinates on various aspects of their duties.
Of the following methods you might use to begin such a program, the one which is likely to be MOST productive is to

    A. express your own ideas and persuade the group to accept them
    B. save time and cover more ground by asking questions calling for yes or no answers
    C. propose to the group a general plan of action rather than specific ideas carefully worked out
    D. provide an informal atmosphere for the exchange of ideas

24. The principle of learning by which a foreman might get the BEST results in training his subordinates is:

    A. Letting the learner discover and correct his own mistakes
    B. Teaching the most technical part of the work first
    C. Teaching all parts of the work during the first training session
    D. Getting the learner to use as many of his five senses as possible

25. A new mechanic is to be trained to do an involved operation containing several steps of varying difficulty. This mechanic will MOST likely learn the operation more quickly if he is taught

    A. each step in its proper order
    B. the hardest steps first
    C. the easiest steps first
    D. first the steps that do not require tools

25.____

KEY (CORRECT ANSWERS)

1. C	11. B
2. B	12. A
3. C	13. D
4. A	14. B
5. B	15. B
6. C	16. C
7. B	17. A
8. A	18. D
9. D	19. A
10. C	20. C

21. A
22. B
23. D
24. D
25. C

TEST 2

DIRECTIONS: Each question or incomplete statement is followed by several suggested answers or completions. Select the one that BEST answers the question or completes the statement. *PRINT THE LETTER OF THE CORRECT ANSWER IN THE SPACE AT THE RIGHT.*

1. The one of the following job situations in which it is better to give a written order than an oral order is when

    A. the job involves many details
    B. you can check the job's progress easily
    C. the job is repetitive in nature
    D. there is an emergency

2. Which one of the following serves as the BEST guideline for you to follow for effective written reports?
Keep sentences

    A. short and limit sentences to one thought
    B. short and use as many thoughts as possible
    C. long and limit sentences to one thought
    D. long and use as many thoughts as possible

3. Of the following, the BEST reason why a foreman generally should not do the work of an individual mechanic is that

    A. the shop's production figures will not be accurate
    B. a foreman is paid to supervise
    C. the foreman must maintain his authority
    D. the employee may become self-conscious

4. One method by which a foreman might prepare written reports to management is to begin with the conclusions, results, or summary and to follow this with the supporting data.
The BEST reason why management may prefer this form of report is because

    A. management lacks the specific training to understand the data
    B. the data completely supports the conclusions
    C. time is saved by getting to the conclusions of the report first
    D. the data contains all the information that is required for making the conclusions

5. Forms used for time records and work orders are important to the work of a foreman PRIMARILY because they give him

    A. the knowledge of and familiarity with work operations
    B. the means of control of personnel, material, or job costs
    C. the means for communicating with other workers
    D. a useful method for making filing procedures easier

6. The one of the following which is the MOST important factor in determining the number of employees you can effectively supervise is the

   A. type of work to be performed
   B. priority of the work to be performed
   C. salary level of the workers
   D. ratio of permanent employees to temporary employees

6.____

7. Of the following, you will be MOST productive in carrying out your supervisory responsibilities if you

   A. are capable of doing the same work as your mechanics
   B. meet with your mechanics frequently
   C. are very friendly with your mechanics
   D. get work done through your mechanics

7.____

8. You have been asked to prepare the annual budget for your maintenance shop.
   The one of the following which is the FIRST step you should take in preparing this budget is to determine the

   A. amount of maintenance work which is scheduled for the shop
   B. time it takes for a specific unit of work to be completed
   C. current workload of each employee in the shop
   D. policies and procedures of the shop's operations

8.____

9. When determining the amount of work you expect a group of mechanics to perform in a given time, the BEST procedure for you to follow should be to

   A. aim for a higher level of production than that of the most productive worker
   B. stay at the present production level
   C. set general instead of specific goals
   D. let workers participate in the determination whenever possible

9.____

10. You have been asked to set next year's performance goals concerning the ratio of jobs completed on schedule to total jobs worked. A review of last year's record shows that the workers completed their jobs on schedule 85% of the time, with the best ones showing an on-time ratio of 92% and the poorest ones showing an on-time ratio of 65%.
    Using these facts in line with generally accepted goal-setting practices, you should set a performance ratio for the next year on the basis of _____ average with a _____ minimum acceptable for any employee.

    A. 85%; 65%   B. 85%; 70%   C. 90%; 65%   D. 90%; 70%

10.____

11. It is important for you to be able to identify the critical parts of a large project such as the remodeling of your maintenance shop.
    The one of the following which is the BEST reason why this is important is that it may

    A. help you to set up good communications between you and your workers
    B. give you a better understanding of the purpose of the project
    C. give you control over the time and cost involved in the project
    D. help you to determine who are your most productive workers

11.____

12. When doing work planning for your shop, the factor that you should normally consider LAST among the following is knowing your

    A. major objectives
    B. record keeping system
    C. minor objectives
    D. priorities

13. You have the responsibility for ordering all materials for your maintenance shop. A listing of materials needed for the operations of your shop is long overdue. You realize that you are unable to find time to take care of the inventory personally because of a high priority project you have been working on which has been taking all of your time. You do not know when you will be finished with the project.
    The BEST of the following courses of action to take in handling this inventory matter is to

    A. request that you be taken off the project immediately so that you may take care of the inventory
    B. complete your high priority project and then do the inventory yourself
    C. volunteer to work overtime so that you may complete the inventory while continuing with the project
    D. assign the inventory work to a competent subordinate

14. You have the authority and responsibility for seeing that proper records are kept in your shop. Assume that you decide to delegate to a records clerk the responsibility for collecting the time sheets and the authority to make changes on the time sheets to correct the information when necessary.
    Of the following, which one is the BEST argument that can be made regarding your decision?

    A. *Unacceptable*; because you can delegate only your responsibility but none of your authority to the records clerk
    B. *Acceptable*; because you can delegate some of your authority and some of your responsibility to the records clerk
    C. *Unacceptable;* because you can delegate only your authority but none of your responsibility to the records clerk
    D. *Acceptable;* because you can delegate all your responsibility and all your authority to the records clerk

15. You will LEAST likely be able to do an effective job of controlling operating costs if you

    A. eliminate idle time
    B. reduce absenteeism
    C. raise your budget
    D. combine work operations

16. Of the following actions, the one which is LEAST likely to help in carrying out your responsibilities of looking after the interests of your workers is to

    A. crack down on your workers when necessary
    B. let your workers know that you support company policy
    C. prevent the transfers of your workers
    D. back up your workers in a controversy

17. The term *accountability*, as used in management of supervision, means MOST NEARLY

    A. responsibility for results
    B. record keeping
    C. bookkeeping systems
    D. inventory control

18. Assume that you have been unable to convince an employee of the seriousness of his poor attendance record by talking to him.
The one of the following which is the BEST course of action for you to take is to

    A. keep talking to the employee
    B. recommend that a written warning be given
    C. consider transferring the employee to another work location
    D. recommend that the employee be fired

19. When delegating work to a subordinate foreman, you should NOT

    A. delegate the right to make any decisions
    B. be interested in the results of the work, but in the method of doing the work
    C. delegate any work that you can do better than your subordinate
    D. give up your final responsibility for the work

20. Of the following statements, the BEST reason why proper scheduling of maintenance work is important is that it

    A. eliminates the need for individual job work orders
    B. classifies job skills in accordance with performance
    C. minimizes lost time in performing any maintenance job
    D. determines needed repairs in various locations

21. Of the following factors, the one which is of LEAST importance in determining the number of subordinates that an individual should be assigned to supervise is the

    A. nature of the work being supervised
    B. qualifications of the individual as a supervisor
    C. capabilities of the subordinates
    D. lines of promotion for the subordinates

22. Suppose that a large number of semi-literate residents of this city have been requesting the assistance of your department. You are asked to prepare a form which these applicants will be required to fill out before their requests will be considered.
In view of these facts, the one of the following factors to which you should give the GREATEST amount of consideration in preparing this form is the

    A. size of the form
    B. sequence of the information asked for on the form
    C. level of difficulty of the language used in the form
    D. number of times which the form will have to be reviewed

23. A budget is a plan whereby a goal is set for future operations. It affords a medium for comparing actual expenditures with planned expenditures.
The one of the following which is the MOST accurate statement on the basis of this statement is that

    A. the budget serves as an accurate measure of past as well as future expenditures
    B. the budget presents an estimate of expenditures to be made in the future
    C. budget estimates should be based upon past budget requirements
    D. planned expenditures usually fall short of actual expenditures

24. A foreman who is familiar with modern management principles should know that the one of the following requirements of an administrator which is LEAST important is his ability to

   A. coordinate work
   B. plan, organize, and direct the work under his control
   C. cooperate with others
   D. perform the duties of the employees under his jurisdiction

25. The one of the following which should be considered the LEAST important objective of the service rating system is to

   A. rate the employees on the basis of their potential abilities
   B. establish a basis for assigning employees to special types of work
   C. provide a means of recognizing superior work performance
   D. reveal the need for training as well as the effectiveness of a training program

KEY (CORRECT ANSWERS)

1.	A	11.	C
2.	A	12.	B
3.	B	13.	D
4.	C	14.	B
5.	B	15.	C
6.	A	16.	C
7.	D	17.	A
8.	A	18.	B
9.	D	19.	D
10.	D	20.	C

21.	D
22.	C
23.	B
24.	D
25.	A

EXAMINATION SECTION
TEST 1

DIRECTIONS: Each question or incomplete statement is followed by several suggested answers or completions. Select the one that BEST answers the question or completes the statement. *PRINT THE LETTER OF THE CORRECT ANSWER IN THE SPACE AT THE RIGHT.*

1. Which of the following substances causes asphalt tile to turn spongy? 1.____

    A. Oil B. Varnish C. Water D. Dust

2. Which of the following would NOT cause asphalt tile to turn yellow? 2.____

    A. A layer of dust B. Varnish
    C. Lacquer D. Water

3. Which one of the following is LEAST likely to be an advantage of waxing a floor? 3.____

    A. Helps to make a room quieter
    B. Helps to reduce wear on the floor
    C. Gives a pleasant shine to the floor
    D. Improves the stain resistance of the floor

4. The action of liquid cleaner on a floor with built-up wax is to 4.____

    A. make the wax disappear into the air
    B. turn the wax into little grains that must be swept up in a vacuum cleaner
    C. soften the wax, which has to be scrubbed away and then rinsed off
    D. make the floor waterproof

5. After how many waxings should built-up wax be removed from a floor? 5.____
Every

    A. waxing B. 3 waxings
    C. 6 waxings D. 12 waxings

6. Manuals on floor cleaning describe methods of cleaning *resilient flooring*. 6.____
Which of the following kinds of flooring surfaces is NOT *resilient*?
_____ tile.

    A. Cork B. Asphalt C. Vinyl D. Terrazzo

7. In buffing a floor, it is NOT desirable to use a polishing brush because the 7.____

    A. brush will scratch the surface you are trying to polish
    B. strands of the brush fall out easily
    C. brush is often used for other purposes
    D. brush does not usually remove deep scuff marks

8. *Rolling* results when only the upper parts of a wax coat dry, leaving the lower parts wet. 8.____
In waxing a floor, this condition comes from

    A. putting on too thick a coat of wax
    B. putting on too thin a coat of wax

25

C. rinsing the floor before applying the wax
D. leaving soap on the floor before applying the wax

9. After a cork or linoleum floor is installed, how long should you wait before you mop the floor for the FIRST time?

   A. 1 day B. 3 days C. 12 hours D. 2 weeks

10. On sweeping stairways, you should direct your men to make a practice of sweeping them

    A. when tenant traffic is heavy, so that people can see them working
    B. whenever they have free time during the day
    C. during the morning at a time when tenant traffic is lightest
    D. in the middle of the day, when the traffic is medium heavy

11. How often must public corridors be swept?

    A. Only when a visible amount of dirt piles up
    B. Every day
    C. Once a week
    D. Every three days

12. You should NOT use an oily mop to sweep any floor because it

    A. leaves a sticky film that can catch dust
    B. eats away at the floor like acid
    C. makes the floor completely waterproof
    D. prevents wax from being applied

13. Which of the following would NOT be used on a concrete floor?

    A. Water base wax   B. Oily sweeping compound
    C. Solvent wax   D. Wire brush

14. You should NOT use an alkaline cleaner on linoleum floors because the cleaner

    A. will make the floor shine too brightly
    B. makes the linoleum sticky
    C. makes the linoleum crack and curl
    D. costs too much to be practical

15. The BEST way of wet mopping a large floor area is to mop the floor area

    A. with a circular motion
    B. from side to side or with a figure 8 motion
    C. with forward and back strokes
    D. alternate side to side and forward and back

16. The type of product to use when cleaning terrazzo floors is

    A. mild cleaner   B. diluted acid solution
    C. scouring powder   D. paste wax

17. A caretaker was met mopping an asphalt tile floor. He decided to make the floor as wet as possible.
For him to do this is a

   A. *good* idea, because the more water you use, the cleaner the floor will be
   B. *bad* idea, because water should never be wasted
   C. *good* idea, because the floor will not have to be washed as often
   D. *bad* idea, because the excess water will eventually damage the floor surface

17._____

18. When you wet clean a stairway by hand, you need two buckets.
One of them is for the cleaning solution, and the other one is used for

   A. extra ammonia for cleaning
   B. rinsing, and should be filled with clean water
   C. putting out fires, and should be filled with sand
   D. storage of equipment

18._____

19. The cleaning of stairways is USUALLY scheduled to be done with

   A. corridor cleaning   B. sidewalk cleaning
   C. incinerator work   D. move-outs

19._____

20. *Dry cleaning* in relation to a building refers to

   A. a reconditioning process that restores the appearance of a floor and protects the surface by buffing
   B. dusting of a wall area with specially treated cloth in order to produce a sheen
   C. patch waxing of a floor with a powdered wax compound
   D. dry mopping only of a floor area

20._____

Questions 21-25.

DIRECTIONS: Questions 21 through 25 are to be answered ONLY according to the information given in the following paragraph.

In order to help prevent the spread of fire, it is necessary to understand the means by which heat is transmitted. Heat is transmitted through solids by a method called *conduction*. Materials vary greatly in their ability to transmit heat. Metals are good conductors of heat. On the other hand, wood, glass, pottery, asbestos, and many like substances are very poor conductors of heat and are termed insulators. It should be remembered, however, that there are no perfect insulators of heat. All will conduct heat to some extent, and if the heat continues long enough, it will be transmitted through the solid. The hazard of heat transmission is illustrated by the fact that a fire on one side of a metal wall could start a fire on the other side if combustibles were close to the wall.

21. Of the following, the BEST material to use for the handle of a metal pan to guard against heat is

   A. copper   B. iron   C. wood   D. steel

21._____

22. According to the above paragraph, *conduction* applies to the traveling of heat through a

   A. solid   B. liquid
   C. slow-moving fluid   D. gas

22._____

23. According to the information in the above paragraph, when storing combustible materials in a room with metal walls, it is BEST to

    A. keep the combustibles close together
    B. keep the combustibles away from the metal walls
    C. put the non-metals nearest the metal walls
    D. separate metal materials from non-metal materials

24. Based on the information in the above paragraph, which one of the following objects is the BEST conductor of heat?

    A. Pottery
    B. An oak desk
    C. A glass jar
    D. A silver spoon

25. Of the following, the title which BEST describes what the above paragraph is about is

    A. Uses of Conductors and Insulators
    B. The Reasons Why Fire Spreads
    C. Heat Transmission and Fires
    D. The Hazards of Poor Conduction

KEY (CORRECT ANSWERS)

1. A
2. A
3. A
4. C
5. C
6. D
7. D
8. A
9. B
10. C
11. B
12. A
13. B
14. C
15. B
16. A
17. D
18. B
19. A
20. A
21. C
22. A
23. B
24. D
25. C

TEST 2

DIRECTIONS: Each question or incomplete statement is followed by several suggested answers or completions. Select the one that BEST answers the question or completes the statement. *PRINT THE LETTER OF THE CORRECT ANSWER IN THE SPACE AT THE RIGHT.*

1. If it is necessary to wash stairways, this should be done during the 1.____

   A. day
   B. night
   C. weekend
   D. morning rush hour

2. A caretaker noticed that a family was moving out. He gave the following information to the foreman: name and apartment number of the family and the van license number. Which one of the following facts did the caretaker leave out that he should have given to the foreman? 2.____

   A. Registration number of the moving van
   B. Inspection date of the moving van
   C. Name of the moving company
   D. Names and addresses of the movers

3. A caretaker sees that a lock on the outside door of a project building has been broken by vandals.
   This should be reported FIRST to the 3.____

   A. housing manager
   B. foreman of caretakers
   C. building superintendent
   D. assistant building superintendent

4. In housing authority practice, a garage broom is *usually* used to sweep 4.____

   A. small asphalt walks
   B. playgrounds
   C. small cement walks
   D. incinerator rooms

5. Listed below, and numbered in scrambled order, are the first four steps to follow when you are dusting furniture: 5.____
   I. Move objects on furniture and dust under them
   II. Refold cloth
   III. Dust furniture itself
   IV. Fold the dusting cloth
   The CORRECT order of these steps should be:

   A. I, IV, III, II
   B. III, IV, II, I
   C. IV, II, I, III
   D. IV, III, II, I

6. Snow removal should begin 6.____

   A. after the snow has been packed solid
   B. as soon as possible
   C. when the depth is more than 2 inches
   D. when the weather bureau says it is a *heavy snowfall*

7. On which of the following should you advise a caretaker to use a corn broom?

   A. Basement areas
   B. Stair halls
   C. Rubber tile floor
   D. Window sills

8. Chrome fixtures should be cleaned by

   A. using a mild soap solution then polishing with a soft cloth
   B. dusting lightly, then wax with oil base wax
   C. polishing with a scouring pad
   D. washing with a solution of water and ammonia, then rinsing with a detergent

9. The MAIN reason caretakers are advised to wear protective goggles while changing a broken bulb is to avoid the danger of

   A. glare from the bulb
   B. pieces of glass getting in the eyes
   C. sparks from the bulb
   D. insects on or around the bulb socket

10. Oily rags should be placed in a container made of

    A. metal
    B. cardboard
    C. cloth
    D. wood

11. When a caretaker lights an incinerator in the morning, the door to the incinerator room should be

    A. all the way open
    B. all the way closed
    C. half-way open, to let the air in
    D. open or closed, depending on the weather

12. Wood and cork floors should be sealed because

    A. these surfaces have tiny natural openings that can trap dirt and grease
    B. it keeps these kinds of floors from warping and buckling
    C. it makes the surface stronger
    D. the sealing process makes the surface easier to walk on

13. A single 8-foot ladder is to be used for a certain window washing job.
    Of the distances from the wall which are given below, which one is BEST to place the ladder from the wall? _____ feet.

    A. 2   B. 4   C. 6   D. 8

14. To lift something without injury to yourself, you should obey all of the following rules EXCEPT:

    A. Keep your back straight
    B. Get help with heavy loads
    C. Lift quickly with your arms
    D. Stand close to what you are lifting

15. The type of product to use when cleaning asphalt tile is 15.____

   A. sandpaper pad
   B. plain ammonia
   C. water base wax
   D. oil base polish

16. When you are taking a mop outfit with wringer through a corridor, it is VERY important to proceed slowly past doorways because 16.____

   A. you might slip and hurt yourself
   B. you should look for any cracks in the floor
   C. you must watch out for people who might come through the doorway
   D. the doorway area is more slippery than the rest of the corridor

17. Which one of the following is the MOST important piece of clothing to wear while cleaning an incinerator? 17.____

   A. Leather boots
   B. Fireman's helmet
   C. Heavy coat
   D. Work gloves

18. Of the following, who should hang the elevator pads to be used when tenants move in or out? 18.____
   The

   A. foreman of housing caretakers
   B. tenant himself
   C. caretaker assigned to the building
   D. elevator mechanic

19. One day a caretaker said to his foreman, *I can get a tile cleaner that is as good as the stuff we use, and for less money, because my brother is a building contractor. How about it?* 19.____
   The CORRECT way for the foreman to handle this situation is for him to

   A. thank the caretaker, but tell him that individual caretakers cannot buy their own cleaning material for project use
   B. tell the caretaker that no one has any right to start interfering in the buying procedures of the housing authority
   C. go along with the caretaker and buy the cleaner from his brother, because it might save money for the authority
   D. tell the caretaker to have his brother contact the project manager

20. A new caretaker under your supervision is waxing a floor for the first time. While the job seems to be going along well, he is not doing it quite the way you asked him to do it and so is taking longer than he should. 20.____
   Which of the following is the BEST action for you to take under these conditions?

   A. Leave him to finish the job and go on to the next one
   B. Interrupt him and tell him to do the job the way he was taught
   C. Tell him he is doing well but that he should do better
   D. Explain to him why your way is faster and tell him to try it

21. The EASIEST way to find out how many supplies you have available is for you to 21.____

   A. look at last year's figures
   B. keep an up-to-date inventory

C. ask one of your men to let you know
D. check the availability when you use a special item

Questions 22-23.

DIRECTIONS: Questions 22 and 23 are to be answered on the basis of information in the following paragraph.

Studies show that the average high-class office building has a tenant population of around 750 persons per 100,000 square feet of area and that the elevators normally have to handle from seven to ten times as many passengers per day as the total number of permanent occupants.

22. Based on the above, what would be the AVERAGE tenant population of a building having 300,000 square feet of space?   22.___

   A. 1,000   B. 2,250   C. 2,200   D. 750

23. Based on the above, how many passengers would the elevator have to handle per day if the area of the building is 100,000 square feet?   23.___
   From

   A. 5,250 to 7,500   B. 750 to 1,500
   C. 1,000 to 2,500   D. 2,500 to 5,000

Questions 24-25.

DIRECTIONS: Questions 24 and 25 are to be answered on the basis of information in the paragraph below.

A large number of studies show that in diversified tenancy buildings, the maximum five-minute morning incoming traffic flow averages 12% of the building population and that the noon peak at its highest five-minute period averages about 15% of the building, population.

24. Based on the above, with a building population of 1,000, how many people would the elevators have to handle during the MAXIMUM incoming morning traffic period?   24.___

   A. 120   B. 130   C. 150   D. 160

25. How many people during the highest five-minute peak period of the noon rush hour would the elevator be able to handle at MAXIMUM capacity with a building population of 1,000?   25.___

   A. 120   B. 125   C. 150   D. 175

KEY (CORRECT ANSWERS)

1.	C	11.	B
2.	C	12.	A
3.	B	13.	A
4.	B	14.	C
5.	D	15.	C
6.	B	16.	C
7.	A	17.	D
8.	A	18.	C
9.	B	19.	A
10.	A	20.	D

21. B
22. B
23. A
24. A
25. C

EXAMINATION SECTION
TEST 1

DIRECTIONS: Each question or incomplete statement is followed by several suggested answers or completions. Select the one that BEST answers the question or completes the statement. *PRINT THE LETTER OF THE CORRECT ANSWER IN THE SPACE AT THE RIGHT.*

1. An instrument that is USUALLY mounted on a boiler control panel and which is read in inches of water is known as a(n) _____ gauge.

    A. pressure
    B. draft
    C. stack temperature
    D. Orsat indicator

2. The type of pump which should be used to supply fuel oil to a low-pressure boiler is the _____ pump.

    A. centrifugal   B. diaphragm   C. rotary gear   D. reciprocating

3. A thermostatic radiator trap which is working satisfactorily will

    A. *open* to pass the steam
    B. *open* to pass the condensate
    C. *close* to retain the cool air
    D. *close* to retain the condensate

4. Readings of stack temperature and percentage of carbon dioxide are useful in the boiler room in determining changes in the boiler's _____ efficiency.

    A. mechanical   B. volumetric   C. overall   D. combustion

5. In the start-up cycle of a boiler which is equipped with all of the following devices, the device that should be energized BEFORE all the others is the

    A. magnetic oil valve
    B. ignition transformer
    C. gas solenoid valve
    D. fresh air louvre motor

6. The one of the following valves which is electrically operated is the _____ valve.

    A. pressure relief
    B. magnetic oil
    C. check
    D. thermostatic control

7. In an installation where there is only one fuel-oil pump set, a duplex strainer is PREFERABLY used because

    A. one side of the strainer can be cleaned without interrupting the flow of oil
    B. one side of the strainer will screen out much finer particles than the other side
    C. the flow of oil can be directed through both sides at the same time, thereby increasing the velocity of the oil
    D. cleaning of a duplex strainer is not required during the heating season

8. A higher-than-normal vacuum reading on a gauge which is attached to the suction side of a fuel-oil pump generally indicates that there is

    A. no oil in the tank
    B. a clogged strainer in the suction line
    C. a broken fitting in the suction line
    D. worn packing on the pump

9. The one of the following which is NOT a possible point of entry of water leaking into the fuel-oil storage tank is the

   A. fuel fill pipe can
   B. sounding well plug
   C. steam coil in a fuel-oil heater
   D. fire box side of the furnace wall

10. When an air vaporstat which is connected to an automatic rotary cup oil burner senses the loss of primary air pressure in the fan housing, it *de-energizes* the

    A. burner motor-starter coil
    B. magnetic-oil valve
    C. secondary air-damper control
    D. modutrol motor

11. A steam boiler which is externally fired and in which the hot gases pass through the tubes is commonly known as a _____ boiler.

    A. Scotch
    B. locomotive
    C. horizontal return tubular
    D. vertical tubular

12. The modulating pressuretrol on an automatic rotary cup oil-fired boiler controls the

    A. modutrol motor circuit
    B. magnetic oil valve
    C. burner motor starter
    D. electric heater

13. The reason for *blowing down* a boiler is to

    A. *lower* the boiler water level below the boiler tubes
    B. *reduce* the concentration of dissolved solids in the boiler water
    C. *reduce* the concentration of dissolved oxygen in the boiler water
    D. *eliminate* the need for treating the boiler water chemically

14. The one of the following boiler pressure-actuated devices which should be adjusted to operate at the highest pre-sure setting is the

    A. pop-safety valve
    B. manual-reset pressuretrol
    C. modulating pressuretrol
    D. limit pressuretrol

15. The BEST procedure for testing the operation of a low-water cutout is to *lower* the _____ until the burner shuts off.

    A. boiler water level *rapidly*
    B. boiler water level *slowly*
    C. water level in the water column *rapidly*
    D. water level in the water column *slowly*

16. If the water disappears from the gauge glass on a low-pressure oil-fired boiler, the FIRST action the boiler operator should take is to

    A. shut off the water
    B. add water to the boiler until the glass fills up to the correct level
    C. open the bottom blow-down valve
    D. blow down the water column

17. On a certain day, the lowest outside temperature was 20° F and the highest was 40° F. The number of degree days for this day is

    A. 25   B. 30   C. 35   D. 45

18. A vacuum return line pump should NOT be operated with the electrical control set for

    A. continuous operation
    B. float and vacuum control
    C. float control only
    D. vacuum control only

19. The PREFERRED location for a Dunham Selector is on the _____ exposure of the building.

    A. north   B. east   C. south   D. west

20. Maintaining a Dunham Heat Balancer in good working order requires *annual* cleaning of its

    A. radiator fins
    B. relay contacts
    C. solenoid valve
    D. fulcrum

21. A chemical useful in reducing the concentration of oxygen in boiler water is

    A. tannin
    B. amines
    C. sodium sulphite
    D. sodium carbonate

22. Smoke alarms which must be installed on oil-fired boilers should create a loud signal and a red flashing light upon the emission of an air contaminant whose density, when compared to the standard smoke chart, appears darker than Number _____ on the chart.

    A. 1   B. 2   C. 3   D. 4

23. Samples for the testing of boiler water should be taken from the

    A. bottom blow-off
    B. condensate tank
    C. water column
    D. condensate-return line

24. In a building which is heated by an oil-fired boiler, 2,100 gallons of fuel oil were burned in a period in which the degree days reached a total of 1,400.
    If all other conditions remained constant, the number of gallons of fuel oil that would be burned in this building during a period in which the degree days reached a total of 3,600 is

    A. 2,400   B. 2,900   C. 4,800   D. 5,400

25. Of the following fuels, the one with the HIGHEST viscosity is

    A. kerosene   B. natural gas   C. #6 oil   D. #2 oil

KEY (CORRECT ANSWERS)

1. B
2. C
3. B
4. D
5. D

6. B
7. A
8. B
9. D
10. B

11. C
12. A
13. B
14. A
15. B

16. A
17. C
18. D
19. A
20. A

21. C
22. A
23. C
24. D
25. C

TEST 2

DIRECTIONS: Each question or incomplete statement is followed by several suggested answers or completions. Select the one that BEST answers the question or completes the statement. *PRINT THE LETTER OF THE CORRECT ANSWER IN THE SPACE AT THE RIGHT.*

1. The device which **protects** the boiler from damage due to low water is the   1._____

   A. fusible plug
   B. fusible link
   C. vaporstat
   D. aquastat

2. In a low-pressure fire-tube boiler, the oil burner should be shut off BEFORE   2._____

   A. operating the soot blower
   B. taking a flue gas sample
   C. blowing down the boiler
   D. blowing down the water column

3. A domestic hot water circulating pump is started and stopped automatically by means of a(n) _____ in the line.   3._____

   A. pressuretrol; supply
   B. pressuretrol; return
   C. aquastat; supply
   D. aquastat; return

4. On a steam-heated domestic hot water generator, the device which acts to *prevent* damage to the coils due to a high internal pressure differential between the coil and the tank is the   4._____

   A. pressure relief valve
   B. vacuum breaker
   C. air vent valve
   D. steam trap

5. In the city, the rules and regulations concerning the cleaning of a water tank which is part of a building's domestic water supply are specified by the   5._____

   A. fire department
   B. department of housing and buildings
   C. city sanitary code
   D. board of water supply

6. A housing fireman, making a preliminary inspection of a fuel oil delivery truck, discovers that the level of the oil in one compartment is far below the marker.
   In this case, he SHOULD   6._____

   A. reject the shipment and order that it be returned to the terminal
   B. measure the level of the oil in the low compartment by *sticking* and report his findings to the superintendent before unloading
   C. read the liquidometer gauge before allowing the truck to be unloaded and again after it has been unloaded and record the difference in gallons to determine the amount for which payment should be made
   D. ignore the low level if it is in only one compartment

7. Of the following fire extinguishers, the one which should be provided for use in the elevator machine room is the _____ type.

   A. carbon dioxide
   B. soda-acid
   C. foam
   D. loaded-stream

8. The wall surface which does NOT have to be washed from the bottom up to avoid streaking is a(n) _____ wall.

   A. semi-gloss painted
   B. enamel painted
   C. glazed tile
   D. unglazed tile

9. The one of the following practices which is GENERALLY recommended to prolong the useful life of a corn broom is

   A. soaking a new broom overnight before using it for the first time to remove brittleness
   B. storing the broom with the tips of the straws resting on the floor to keep the edges even
   C. keeping the straws moistened when sweeping
   D. storing the broom in a warm humid enclosure to prevent drying of the bristles

10. While a caretaker is sweeping the public corridors and stairways, he notices some crayon marks on walls and stains on the floors.
    He SHOULD

    A. stop sweeping and remove the stains immediately
    B. finish sweeping and then return to remove the stains
    C. make note of the marks and stains in his building and remove them once a month
    D. make a note of the marks and stains and report them to the superintendent so that the cause can be eliminated before the stains are removed

11. When transporting the equipment required for mopping stairhalls and corridors, a caretaker should NOT

    A. attempt to do it alone
    B. carry water in the pails because spillage may cause a tenant to slip and fall
    C. use the elevator
    D. carry the equipment in both hands when climbing stairs

12. A caretaker should apply washing solution to a portion of a painted wall and should rinse the same area before applying the solution to another area.
    In order to allow sufficient time for the solution to take effect on the soil, the area covered each time should be APPROXIMATELY _____ square feet.

    A. 20   B. 60   C. 160   D. 600

13. Asphalt tile floors should be maintained by coating them with

    A. water emulsion wax
    B. paste wax
    C. oil emulsion wax
    D. neat's-foot oil

14. The broom with which a caretaker should sweep an asphalt-paved playground is the _____ broom.

    A. hair   B. corn   C. garage   D. Scotch

15. A paper sticker should be used by a caretaker to

 A. pick up litter and fruit skins
 B. make temporary warning signs to be placed around wet floor areas
 C. indicate on the elevator panel on which floor he is working
 D. feed old newspapers into the incinerator

16. The type of floor which should be cleaned by sweeping and then mopping with an abrasive detergent is the _____ floor.

 A. painted cement
 B. unpainted cement
 C. asphalt tile
 D. terrazzo

17. The term *cutting the water* refers to one step in the procedure for

 A. cleaning windows
 B. treating boiler water
 C. watering lawns
 D. washing walls

18. Stains on ceramic tile may be removed by very carefully using a dilute solution of _____ acid.

 A. acetic
 B. oxalic
 C. sulphuric
 D. hydrochloric

19. The directions on the label of a bottle of detergent call for mixing four ounces of detergent with one gallon of water to make a cleaning solution for washing floors.
In order to obtain a LARGER amount of solution of the same strength, one quart of the detergent should be mixed with _____ gallons of water.

 A. 2   B. 4   C. 6   D. 8

20. Garden soil which has a pH reading of 6.0 is said to be

 A. neutral
 B. slightly acid
 C. slightly alkaline
 D. strongly acid

21. Acid soil can be treated so that the acidity is reduced by using

 A. limestone
 B. peat moss
 C. humus
 D. nitrogen

22. The one of the following procedures which is NOT recommended for growing turfgrass in shaded areas is to

 A. fertilize more frequently than normal
 B. water deeply and frequently
 C. compact the soil as much as possible
 D. prune shallow tree roots as much as possible

23. Hedges should be trimmed so that the top is _____ than the bottom with the solid leaf growth starting _____ the ground.

 A. *narrower;* about eighteen inches above
 B. *narrower;* as close as possible to
 C. *wider;* about eighteen inches above
 D. *wider;* as close as possible to

24. A checklist of outdoor tasks which should be performed in March and April should NOT include

   A. fertilizing lawn areas
   B. applying dormant spray
   C. cleaning window wells
   D. spraying broad-leaved weeds

25. Lawns should be mowed when the grass has attained a height of _____ inch(es) with the mower set at _____ inch(es).

   A. 4; 3   B. 3; 2   C. 2; 1   D. 1; 1/2

KEY (CORRECT ANSWERS)

1. A	11. D
2. C	12. C
3. D	13. A
4. B	14. C
5. C	15. A
6. B	16. B
7. A	17. A
8. C	18. D
9. A	19. D
10. B	20. B

21. A
22. C
23. B
24. D
25. B

TEST 3

DIRECTIONS: Each question or incomplete statement is followed by several suggested answers or completions. Select the one that BEST answers the question or completes the statement. *PRINT THE LETTER OF THE CORRECT ANSWER IN THE SPACE AT THE RIGHT.*

1. The number of employees required for raising the national flag in the morning and lowering it at night is: 1.____
   _____ employee(s) to raise; _____ employee(s) to lower and fold it.
   A. One; one   B. One; two   C. Two; two   D. Two; one

2. The component of fertilizers which aids in keeping grass from turning brown in the summer time is 2.____
   A. limestone   B. calcium   C. chlordane   D. nitrogen

3. The one of the following chemicals which can be used to melt ice on sidewalks is 3.____
   A. carbon tetrachloride   B. methane
   C. acetic acid   D. sodium chloride

4. A snow fence, which is used to prevent the drifting of snow over certain areas, is USUALLY made of 4.____
   A. wood slats wired together
   B. plastic-coated woven wire
   C. compacted snow
   D. two horizontal wood rails joining vertical posts

5. The area of a lawn which is 58 feet wide by 96 feet long is MOST NEARLY _____ square feet. 5.____
   A. 5000   B. 5500   C. 6000   D. 6500

6. All elevators must be inspected by the department of 6.____
   A. buildings   B. air resources
   C. health   D. labor

7. The training of personnel in the procedure for restoring stalled elevators to service and releasing passengers from stalled elevators should be given by the 7.____
   A. project superintendent
   B. chief superintendent
   C. project elevator mechanic
   D. project assistant superintendent

8. When a maintenance man is greasing a ball bearing pillow block which is equipped with shaft seals, he should pump grease through the grease fitting UNTIL 8.____
   A. a strong back pressure is felt on the gun
   B. grease starts to leak past both seals
   C. clean grease starts to leak out of the opened drain hole
   D. six strokes of the gun handle are counted

9. In buildings, safety checks of every elevator hatch door should be made each day by the

   A. caretaker
   B. elevator mechanic
   C. assistant superintendent
   D. maintenance man

10. The BEST way to find a Freon 12 refrigerant leak in a domestic refrigerator is by using a

    A. sulphur match
    B. plumber's candle
    C. peroxide bath
    D. halide torch

11. Good preventive maintenance of mechanical equipment in a housing project should result in an INCREASE in the

    A. frequency of unscheduled repairs
    B. overall cost of maintenance
    C. down-time of the equipment
    D. efficiency of service

12. In a building, plexiglass can be used to replace ordinary glass which is located in

    A. apartments that are more than 150 feet above curb level
    B. stairhalls
    C. front entrance doors
    D. fire-resistive opening protective assemblies

13. The BEST bit to use in an electric drill when drilling a hole in masonry is a(n)

    A. high-speed steel bit
    B. auger
    C. carbide-tipped bit
    D. tapered-shank tool steel bit

14. The type of fastener used to attach a butt hinge to a metal door is a

    A. round head rivet
    B. flat head machine screw
    C. filister head cap screw
    D. flat head wood screw

15. Burner gas cocks on kitchen stoves should be lubricated when necessary with

    A. refrigerant oil
    B. graphited grease
    C. penetrating oil
    D. cutting oil

16. A type of portable tool used to bend electrical conduit is called a

    A. helve   B. newel   C. spandrel   D. hickey

17. A device used to guide a handsaw to cut boards at a desired angle to form an evenly divided angle joint is called a

    A. miter box   B. backsaw   C. try square   D. protractor

18. The criteria governing preventive maintenance of vehicles require that all of the following be done at certain intervals.
    The one which must be done MOST frequently is

    A. changing the engine oil
    B. changing the engine oil filter
    C. checking the radiator coolant level
    D. rotating the tires

19. Only the plug on the electric cord of a refrigerator gets very hot when the refrigerator is operating normally. The MOST likely cause of this is that there is a(n)

    A. poor electrical connection in the plug
    B. oversized fuse in the circuit
    C. short circuit in the plug
    D. short circuit in the motor

20. Of two back-to-back plumbing fixtures are stopped up at the same time, the stoppage is MOST likely in the

    A. trap of one of the fixtures
    B. waste line in the wall
    C. vent line in the wall
    D. vacuum breaker

21. The procedure which should be followed to stop a faucet drip in a faucet which is equipped with non-renewable seats is to replace

    A. the faucet with a new one
    B. all the washers and seats with new ones
    C. all the washers with new ones and grind the seats until smooth
    D. both spindles

22. The ADVANTAGE of using a flexible coupling over using a rigid coupling on the shaft of a house pump is that the flexible coupling

    A. allows for slight misalignment of the shafts
    B. can transmit more power than a rigid coupling
    C. provides a cushioned start
    D. prevents overloading of the motor

23. The one of the following attitudes which a good supervisor should encourage among his subordinates is that they

    A. should want to do the best possible job
    B. should work only well enough to get by
    C. do not work as hard as the workers in other projects
    D. must produce more work each day than they did on the previous day

24. The supervisory function which deals with the determination of what work a supervisor wants done by his staff is known as

    A. planning   B. staffing
    C. directing   D. controlling

25. The one of the following personality traits that is UNDESIRABLE is

    A. self-confidence   B. intelligence
    C. initiative   D. indifference

KEY (CORRECT ANSWERS)

1. B
2. D
3. D
4. A
5. B

6. A
7. C
8. C
9. A
10. D

11. D
12. C
13. C
14. B
15. B

16. D
17. A
18. C
19. A
20. B

21. C
22. A
23. A
24. A
25. D

EXAMINATION SECTION
TEST 1

DIRECTIONS: Each question or incomplete statement is followed by several suggested answers or completions. Select the one that BEST answers the question or completes the statement. *PRINT THE LETTER OF THE CORRECT ANSWER IN THE SPACE AT THE RIGHT.*

1. The MAIN function of a *steam separator* in a steam power plant is to

    A. reduce steam pressure
    B. remove excess oil vapors from the steam
    C. increase steam quality
    D. reduce back-pressure on the steam-driven equipment

2. The MAIN purpose of a *dip tube* in a low-pressure hot water system is to

    A. prevent air from entering the main
    B. determine the level of water in the boiler
    C. reduce air pollution
    D. eliminate condensation when starting up

3. The rating of a unit ventilator is USUALLY determined by a(n)

    A. anemometer   B. hydrometer
    C. psychrometer   D. ammeter

4. Of the following devices, the one that is used to record the air-flow-steam-flow relationship of a boiler in a steam plant is a

    A. Orsat analyzer   B. manometer
    C. steam-flow meter   D. heat meter

5. Of the following types of gas fuels, the one which has the HIGHEST BTU content per cubic foot is _____ gas.

    A. manufactured   B. coke-oven
    C. liquid petroleum   D. natural

6. Of the following gasket materials, the one which is BEST to use when oil at 300° F is being carried in a pipe is

    A. fiber and paper   B. synthetic rubber
    C. asbestos composition   D. corrugated copper

7. A monolithic repair of a slightly damaged sectional magnesia insulation covering is BEST made by

    A. wiring in a *Dutchman* and filling the voids with magnesia cement
    B. covering the damaged area with asbestos laminations
    C. filling in the broken portion with glass-fiber insulating cement
    D. replacing the entire section

8. Of the following piping materials, the one that should NOT be used in a fuel-oil piping system is

   A. galvanized iron
   B. type K copper tubing
   C. brass pipe
   D. steel pipe

9. A valve is marked *300 WOG.*
   This valve could NOT be properly used in a pipe conveying _____ pounds gage maximum.

   A. oil at 300
   B. air at 100
   C. water at 150
   D. steam at 300

10. A steam gage connection for a large boiler is connected to the top of the water column and is then brought down to the operating level 24 feet below. The gage actually reads 605 psi.
    The ACTUAL gage pressure in the boiler is MOST NEARLY _____ psi.

    A. 590   B. 595   C. 610   D. 620

11. Of the following types of industrial oil burners, the one that is COMPLETELY adaptable to fully automatic operation or wide variations in firing rate is the _____ burner.

    A. mechanical-pressure type
    B. air-atomizing
    C. steam-atomizing
    D. horizontal rotary-cup

12. A full backward curve type centrifugal fan is being used in a coal-fired power plant for forced draft. Assume that after adjusting the speed of the fan, it is still too high, resulting in more pressure than is necessary to overcome the resistance of the fuel bed and boiler. To correct this situation, it would be BEST to replace the fan with one of a _____ diameter, running at _____ rpm and with a _____ wheel.

    A. *smaller;* greater; wider
    B. *larger;* less; wider
    C. *larger;* greater; smaller
    D. *smaller;* less; smaller

13. Short stroking in a steam-driven reciprocating pump results in both a(n) _____ in steam consumption and a(n) _____ in pumping capacity.

    A. *decrease;* decrease
    B. *increase;* increase
    C. *decrease;* increase
    D. *increase;* decrease

14. Caustic embrittlement is the weakening of boiler steel as the result of inner crystalline cracks.
    This condition is caused by BOTH long exposure to

    A. a combination of stress and highly acidic water
    B. stress in the presence of free oxygen and highly acidic water
    C. a combination of stress and water with a pH of 7
    D. a combination of stress and highly alkaline water

15. Of the following statements pertaining to feedwater injectors, the one which is MOST nearly correct is that the injectors

    A. are very efficient pumping units
    B. are practical only on small boilers
    C. are very reliable in operation on all types of boilers
    D. can handle 250 to 300 degree water

    15.____

16. In reference to power plant pumps, the letters N.P.S.H. are an abbreviation for

    A. Non Positive Static Head
    B. Net Position Static Head
    C. Non Positive Standard Head
    D. Net Positive Suction Head

    16.____

17. A pump's maintenance is based on a preventive maintenance schedule. This means that the schedule should GENERALLY be determined by the

    A. actual time lapse between maintenance checks
    B. actual number of pump-operating hours
    C. pump's actual operating performance
    D. operating performance of the equipment connected to the pump

    17.____

18. Periodic inspection and testing of mechanical equipment by the staff at a plant is done MAINLY to

    A. help the men to better understand the operation of the equipment
    B. keep the men busy during slack times
    C. encourage the men to better understand each others' working capabilities
    D. discover minor equipment faults before they develop into major breakdowns

    18.____

19. In planning a preventive maintenance program, the FIRST step to be taken is to

    A. repair all equipment that is not in service
    B. check all fuel oil burner tips
    C. make an inventory of all plant equipment
    D. check all electrical wiring to motors

    19.____

20. An electric motor having class A insulation has been permitted to operate continuously at rated load even though the internal insulation temperature reads 10C above the allowable maximum internal temperature. Operating at this excessive temperature WOULD

    A. require frequent lubrication of the motor bearings
    B. reduce the life expectancy of the electric motor
    C. require an increase in voltage
    D. reduce the power factor to one-half of its normal value

    20.____

21. The synchronous speed of a three-phase squirrel cage induction motor operating from a fixed frequency system can ONLY be changed by altering the

    A. rated locked-rotor torque
    B. rheostat position of the unloaded machine
    C. brush holder position
    D. number of poles in the stator

    21.____

22. A thermal overload relay on an electric motor has been frequently tripping out. Of the following actions, the BEST one to take first to correct this problem would be to

    A. bypass the relay
    B. block the relay on a closed position
    C. clean the relay contacts
    D. arbitrarily readjust the relay setting

23. An air heater for a steam generator providing combustion air at temperatures ranging upward from 300F will often effect savings in fuel ranging from

    A. 1 to 3%   B. 5 to 10%   C. 12 to 15%   D. 17 to 20%

24. You have been asked to make an inspection of the superheater of a steam generator for external corrosion. You should be aware that if the direction of gas flow perpendicular to a tangent to the superheater tube is considered to be the 12 o'clock position, the GREATEST metal loss due to external corrosion usually occurs on the _____ o'clock and _____ o'clock sectors of the tube.

    A. 12; 6   B. 10; 2   C. 8; 3   D. 7; 5

25. In the steam generating plant to which you are assigned, the starting-up time and the shutting-down time for the boiler is determined by the time required to limit the thermal stresses in the drums and headers. The drums and headers have rolled tube joints. The temperature change in saturated temperature per hour for limit controlled heating and cooling rates for this boiler is established at _____ change.

    A. 50° F   B. 75° F   C. 100° F   D. 200° F

KEY (CORRECT ANSWERS)

1. C		11. D	
2. A		12. B	
3. A		13. D	
4. C		14. D	
5. C		15. B	
6. C		16. D	
7. A		17. B	
8. A		18. D	
9. D		19. C	
10. B		20. B	

21. D
22. C
23. B
24. B
25. C

TEST 2

DIRECTIONS: Each question or incomplete statement is followed by several suggested answers or completions. Select the one that BEST answers the question or completes the statement. *PRINT THE LETTER OF THE CORRECT ANSWER IN THE SPACE AT THE RIGHT.*

1. Assume that the optimum pH level of boiler feedwater for a boiler installation ranges between 8.0 and 9.5.
   The alkalizer used in the feedwater treatment to maintain this optimum pH level SHOULD introduce

   A. an average amount of iron and copper corrosion products into the steam cycle
   B. an increase of partial pressure of the carbon dioxide in the steam
   C. the least amount of iron and copper corrosion products into the boiler cycle
   D. a control of corrosion rates by forming a coating on the surfaces contacted by the steam

   1.____

2. The ppm of sodium sulfite that can be *safely* used for the chemical scavenging of oxygen in boiler feedwater is DEPENDENT upon the

   A. steam output of the boiler
   B. boiler operating pressure
   C. number of boiler steam drums
   D. construction of the boiler

   2.____

3. Of the following piping materials, the one which is NOT generally used for pneumatic temperature control systems is

   A. copper   B. plastic
   C. steel   D. galvanized iron

   3.____

4. In accordance with recommended maintenance practice, thermostats used in a pneumatic temperature control system SHOULD be checked

   A. weekly   B. bi-monthly
   C. monthly   D. once a year

   4.____

5. Of the following, the BEST method to use to determine the moisture level in a refrigeration system is to

   A. weigh the drier after it has been in the system for a period of time
   B. visually check the sight glass for particles of corrosion
   C. use a moisture indicator
   D. test a sample of lubricating oil with phosphorus pentoxide

   5.____

6. A full-flow drier is USUALLY recommended to be used in a hermetic refrigeration compressor system to keep the system dry and to

   A. prevent the products of decomposition from getting into the evaporator in the event of a motor burn-out
   B. condense cut liquid refrigerant during compressor off cycles and compressor start-up
   C. prevent the compressor unit from decreasing in capacity
   D. prevent the liquid from dumping into the compressor crankcase

   6.____

7. An economizer in a steam boiler is used to raise the temperature of the

   A. combustion air for firing fuel oil utilizing some of the heat in the exit flue gases
   B. combustion air for firing fuel oil utilizing some of the heat in the exhaust steam from the turbines of steam engines
   C. boiler feedwater by utilizing some of the heat in the exit flue gases
   D. boiler feedwater by utilizing some of the heat in the exhaust steam from the turbines or steam engines

8. A mixed-base grease is a grease that is prepared by mixing lubricating oil with

   A. one metallic soap
   B. two metallic soaps
   C. a synthetic lubricant
   D. heavy gear oil

9. Of the following lubricants, the one which is classified as a circulating oil is _____ oil.

   A. turbine
   B. gear
   C. machine
   D. steam-cylinder

10. You are supervising the installation of a steam-driven reciprocating pump. The pump's air chamber is missing and you have to replace it with one with several salvaged ones. The salvaged air chamber selected should have a volume equal to MOST NEARLY _____ the piston displacement of the pump.

    A. half of
    B. 1 1/2 times
    C. 2 times
    D. 2 1/2 times

11. Economical partial-load operation of steam turbines is obtained by minimizing throttling losses.
    This is accomplished by

    A. reducing the boiler pressure and temperature
    B. throttling the steam flow into the uncontrolled set of nozzles
    C. dividing the first-stage nozzles into several groups and providing a steam control valve for each group
    D. controlling the fuel flow to the steam generator

12. You are ordering two pump wearing rings for a centrifugal pump.
    These rings are GENERALLY identified as

    A. two wearing rings
    B. one drive wearing ring and one casing wearing ring
    C. one casing wearing ring and one impeller wearing ring
    D. one first-stage wearing ring and one drive wearing ring

13. A thermo-hydraulic feedwater regulator is used to regulate the flow of water to a drum-type boiler. The amount of water input to the boiler is controlled *in proportion to* the

    A. boiler load
    B. setting of the feed pump relief valve
    C. amount of water in the outer tube that flashes into steam
    D. water level in the drum

14. The standard capacity rating conditions for any refrigeration compressor is _____ psig for the suction and _____ psig for the discharge.

    A. 5° F, 19.6; 86° F, 154.5 B. 5° F, 9.6; 96° F, 154.5
    C. 10° F, 9.6; 96° F, 144.5 D. 10° F, 19.6; 96° F, 134.5

15. Of the following, the MAIN purpose of a subcooler in a refrigerant piping system for a two-stage system is to

    A. reduce the total power requirements and total heat rejection to the second stage
    B. reduce total power requirements and return oil to the compressor
    C. improve the flow of evaporator gas per ton and increase the temperature
    D. increase the heat rejection per ton and avoid system shutdown

16. In large refrigeration systems, the USUAL location for charging the refrigeration system is into the

    A. suction line
    B. liquid line between the receiver shut-off valve and the expansion valve
    C. line between the condenser and the compressor
    D. line between the high pressure cut-off switch and the expansion valve

17. The effect of a voltage variation to 90 percent of normal voltage, for a compound wound DC motor, on the FULL load current is

    A. an increase in the full load current of approximately 10%
    B. a decrease in the full load current of approximately 10%
    C. zero
    D. a decrease in the full load current 20%

18. The purpose of a current-limiting reactor is to place an upper limit on the available short-circuit current that can occur under fault conditions.
    The reactor accomplishes this by contributing _____ to the circuit.

    A. additional capacitance
    B. reduced inductive reactance
    C. reduced capacitance
    D. additional inductive reactance

19. Alternating current electric motors are usually guaranteed to operate satisfactorily and to deliver their full horsepower PROVIDED the electrical power delivered to the motor is at the rated

    A. voltage and at plus or minus 5 percent frequency variation
    B. frequency and at a voltage 15 percent above or below rating
    C. voltage and at plus or minus 10 percent frequency variation
    D. frequency and at a voltage 20 percent above or below rating

20. A three-phase AC motor is connected to a 230 volt, three-phase, alternating current line. With this motor running at full load, the line current is found to be 20 amperes, with a power factor of 0.75.
    Under these conditions, the power, in kilowatts, supplied to this motor will be MOST NEARLY

    A. 3.5   B. 6.0   C. 10.5   D. 18.0

21. In accordance with the air pollution control code, no person shall cause or permit the emission of air contaminants from a boiler with a capacity of 500 million BTU per hour or more, if the air contaminant emitted has a sulfur dioxide content of MORE than _____ parts per million by volume of undiluted emissions measured at _____ percent excess air.

    A. 300; 15   B. 200; 10   C. 200; 15   D. 300; 10

21.___

22. Of the following statements concerning the requirements of the air pollution control code, the one which is the MOST complete and correct is that the owner of equipment

    A. and apparatus shall maintain such equipment and apparatus in good operating order by regular inspection and cleaning and by promptly making repairs
    B. shall maintain the equipment in good operating condition by making inspections and repairs on a regular basis
    C. and apparatus shall maintain the equipment and apparatus in operating condition by regular inspection and cleaning
    D. shall maintain such equipment in good working order by regular inspection and cleaning and by making repairs on a scheduled basis

22.___

23. Assume that one of your assistants was near the Freon 11 refrigeration system when a liquid Freon line ruptured. Some of the liquid Freon 11 has gotten into your assistant's right eye.
    Of the following actions, the one which you should NOT take is to

    A. immediately call for an eye specialist (medical doctor)
    B. gently and quickly rub the Freon 11 out of the eye
    C. use a boric-acid solution to clean out the Freon 11 from his eye
    D. wash the eye by gently blowing the Freon 11 out of his eye with air

23.___

24. Assume that a fire breaks out in an electrical control panel board.
    Of the following types of portable fire extinguishers, the BEST one to use to put out this fire would be a _____ type.

    A. dry-chemical   B. soda-acid
    C. foam   D. water-stream

24.___

25. Assume that you are checking the water level in a boiler which is on the line in a power plant. Upon opening the gage cocks, you determine that the water level was above the top gage cock.
    Of the following actions, the BEST one to take FIRST in this situation would be to

    A. shut off the fuel and air supply
    B. surface-blow the boiler
    C. close the steam-outlet valve from the boiler
    D. increase the speed of the feedwater pump

25.___

KEY (CORRECT ANSWERS)

1.	C	11.	C
2.	B	12.	C
3.	C	13.	D
4.	D	14.	A
5.	C	15.	A
6.	A	16.	B
7.	C	17.	A
8.	B	18.	D
9.	A	19.	A
10.	D	20.	B

21. B
22. A
23. B
24. A
25. C

EXAMINATION SECTION
TEST 1

DIRECTIONS: Each question or incomplete statement is followed by several suggested answers or completions. Select the one that BEST answers the question or completes the statement. *PRINT THE LETTER OF THE CORRECT ANSWER IN THE SPACE AT THE RIGHT.*

1. The specification states: *The value of each change order shall be computed separately by cost of labor and materials, plus equipment allowance, plus overhead and profit.* The MOST probable value of overhead and profit is _____% of the cost of labor and materials plus equipment allowance.

    A. 5   B. 15   C. 34   D. 55

    1._____

2. In the specifications is an item: *Equipment Allowance: Shall include rental of necessary equipment plus 9% of this rental.*
    According to the above specification, if a piece of equipment rents for $35 per day, Equipment Allowance for this equipment rented for 11 days is MOST NEARLY

    A. $484.00   B. $378.42   C. $385.00   D. $419.65

    2._____

3. A supplier quotes a list price of $172.00 less 15 and 10 percent for twelve tools. The ACTUAL cost for these twelve tools is MOST NEARLY

    A. $146   B. $132   C. $129   D. $112

    3._____

4. Which one of the following is the PRIMARY object in drawing up a set of specifications for materials to be purchased?

    A. Control of quality
    B. Outline of intended use
    C. Establishment of standard sizes
    D. Location and method of inspection

    4._____

5. In order to avoid disputes over payments for extra work in a contract for construction, the BEST procedure to follow would be to

    A. have contractor submit work progress reports daily
    B. insert a special clause in the contract specifications
    C. have a representative on the job at all times to verify conditions
    D. allocate a certain percentage of the cost of the job to cover such expenses

    5._____

6. You wish to order sponges in the most economical manner. Keeping in mind that large sponges can be cut up into many smaller sizes, the one of the following that has the LEAST cost per cubic inch of sponge is _____ sponges @ _____.

    A. 2" x 4" x 6"; $.24
    B. 4" x 8" x 12"; $1.44
    C. 4" x 6" x 36"; $4.80
    D. 6" x 8" x 32"; $9.60

    6._____

7. The cost of a certain job is broken down as follows:
   Materials $375
   Rental of equipment   120
   Labor   315
   The percentage of the total cost of the job that can be charged to materials is MOST NEARLY _____%.

   A. 40 B. 42 C. 44 D. 46

8. Partial payments to outside contractors are USUALLY based on the

   A. breakdown estimate submitted after the contract was signed
   B. actual cost of labor and material plus overhead and profit
   C. estimate of work completed which is generally submitted periodically
   D. estimate of material delivered to the job

9. Building contracts usually require that estimates for changes made in the field be submitted for approval before the work can start.
   The MAIN reason for this requirement is to

   A. make sure that the contractor understands the change
   B. discourage such changes
   C. keep the contractor honest
   D. enable the department to control its expenses

10. If the cost of a broom went up from $4.00 to $6.00, the percent INCREASE in the original cost is

    A. 20 B. 25 C. 33 1/3 D. 50

11. The AVERAGE of the numbers 3, 5, 7, 8, 12 is

    A. 5 B. 6 C. 7 D. 8

12. The cost of 100 bags of cotton cleaning cloths, 89 pounds per bag, at 7 cents per pound is

    A. $549.35 B. $623.00 C. $700.00 D. $890.00

13. If 5 1/2 bags of sweeping compound cost $55,00, then 6 1/2 bags would cost

    A. $60.00 B. $62.50 C. $65.00 D. $67.00

14. The cost of cleaning supplies in a project averaged $330.00 a month during the first 8 months of the year.
    How much can be spent each month for the last four months if the total amount that can be spent for cleaning supplies for the year is $3,880?

    A. $124 B. $220 C. $310 D. $330

15. The cost of rawl plugs is $2.75 per gross. The cost of 2,448 rawl plugs is

    A. $46.75 B. $47.25 C. $47.75 D. $48.25

16. A caretaker received $70.00 for having worked from Monday through Friday, 9 A.M. to 5 P.M. with one hour a day for lunch.
    The number of hours the caretaker would have to work to earn $12.00 is

    A. 10
    B. 6
    C. 70 divided by 12
    D. 70 minus 12

17. Assume that an employee is paid at the rate of $5.43 per hour with time and a half for overtime past 40 hours in a week.
    If he works 43 hours in a week, his gross weekly pay is

    A. $217.20   B. $219.20   C. $229.59   D. $241.64

18. Kerosene costs 36 cents a quart.
    At that rate, two gallons would cost

    A. $1.44   B. $2.16   C. $2.88   D. $3.60

Questions 19-21.

DIRECTIONS: Questions 19 through 21 are to be answered on the basis of the following table.

	Man Days Borough 1		Man Days Borough 2		Man Days Borough 3		Man Days Borough 4	
	Oct.	Nov.	Oct.	Nov.	Oct.	Nov.	Oct.	Nov.
Carpenter	70	100	35	180	145	205	120	85
Plumber	95	135	195	100	70	130	135	80
House Painter	90	90	120	80	85	85	95	195
Electrician	120	110	135	155	120	95	70	205
Blacksmith	125	145	60	180	205	145	80	125

19. In accordance with the above table, if the average daily pay of the five trades listed above is $47.50, the approximate labor cost of work done by the five trades during the month of October for Borough 1 is MOST NEARLY

    A. $22,800   B. $23,450   C. $23,750   D. $26,125

20. In accordance with the above table, the Borough which MOST NEARLY made up 22.4% of the total plumbing work force for the month of November is Borough

    A. 1   B. 2   C. 3   D. 4

21. In accordance with the above table, the average man days per month per Borough spent on electrical work for all Boroughs combined is MOST NEARLY

    A. 120   B. 126   C. 130   D. 136

22. When preparing an estimate for a certain repair job, you determine that $125 worth of materials and 220 man-hours are required to complete the job.
    If your man-hour cost is $5.25 per hour, the TOTAL cost of this repair job is

    A. $1,030   B. $1,155   C. $1,280   D. $1,405

23. Assume that in determining the total cost of a repair job, a 15% shop cost is to be added to the costs of material and labor.
    For a repair job which cost $200 in materials and $600 in labor, the shop cost is

    A. $30   B. $60   C. $90   D. $120

24. Assume that in quantity purchases, the city receives a discount of 33 1/3%.
    If a one gallon can of paint retails at $5.33 per gallon, the cost of 375 gallons of this paint is MOST NEARLY

    A. $1,332.50   B. $1,332.75   C. $1,333.00   D. $1,333.25

25. Assume that eight barrels of cement together weigh a total of 3004 lbs. and 12 oz.
    If there are four bags of cement per barrel, then the weight of one bag of cement is HOST NEARLY _____ lbs.

    A. 93.1   B. 93.5   C. 93.9   D. 94.3

26. Lumber is usually sold by the board foot, and a board foot is defined as a board one foot square and one inch thick.
    If the price of one board foot of lumber is 18 cents and you need 20 feet of lumber 6 inches wide and 1 inch thick, the cost of the 20 feet of lumber is

    A. $1.80   B. $2.40   C. $3.60   D. $4.80

27. Assume that a trench is 42" wide, 5' deep, and 100' long. If the unit price of excavating the trench is $35 per cubic yard, the cost of excavating the trench is MOST NEARLY

    A. $2,275   B. $5,110   C. $7,000   D. $21,000

28. No single activity has a very large effect on the final price of the complete housing structure and, therefore, the total cost is not affected appreciably by the price policy of any component.
    From the above statement, you may conclude that

    A. we cannot hope for substantial reductions in housing costs
    B. the builder must assume responsibility for the high cost of construction
    C. a 10% reduction in the cost of materials would result in much less than a 10% reduction in the cost of housing
    D. federal government financing would reduce the city's cost of public housing

29. Four board feet of lumber, listed at $350 per M, will cost

    A. $3.50   B. $1.40   C. $1.80   D. $4.00

30. The cost of material is approximately 3/8ths of the total cost of a certain job.
    If the total cost of the job is $127.56, then the cost of material is MOST NEARLY

    A. $47.83   B. $48.24   C. $48.65   D. $49.06

31. It takes four men six days to do a certain job. Working at the same speed, the number of days it will take three men to do this job is

    A. 7   B. 8   C. 9   D. 10

32. A contractor on a large construction project USUALLY receives partial payments based on

   A. estimates of completed work
   B. actual cost of materials delivered and work completed
   C. estimates of material delivered and not paid for by the contractor
   D. the breakdown estimate submitted after the contract was signed and prorated over the estimated duration of the contract

33. In estimating the cost of a reinforced concrete structure, the contractor would be LEAST concerned with

   A. volume of concrete
   B. surface area of forms
   C. pounds of reinforcing steel
   D. type of coarse aggregate

34. Assume that an employee is paid at the rate of $6.25 per hour with time and a half for overtime past 40 hours in a week.
    If she works 45 hours in a week, her gross weekly pay is

   A. $285.49   B. $296.88   C. $301.44   D. $325.49

35. Cleaning fluid costs $1.19 a quart.
    If there is a 10% discount for purchases over 5 gallons, how much will 8 gallons cost?

   A. $34.28   B. $38.08   C. $42.28   D. $43.43

KEY (CORRECT ANSWERS)

1. B	11. C	26. A
2. D	12. B	27. A
3. B	13. C	28. C
4. A	14. C	29. B
5. C	15. A	30. A
6. B	16. B	31. B
7. D	17. D	32. A
8. C	18. C	33. D
9. D	19. C	34. B
10. D	20. B	35. A
	21. B	
	22. C	
	23. D	
	24. A	
	25. C	

TEST 2

DIRECTIONS: Each question or incomplete statement is followed by several suggested answers or completions. Select the one that BEST answers the question or completes the statement. *PRINT THE LETTER OF THE CORRECT ANSWER IN THE SPACE AT THE RIGHT.*

1. When windows are mounted side by side, the vertical piece between them is called the

    A. muntin   B. casement   C. sash   D. mullion

    1.___

2. Approximately how many pounds of 16d nails would be required for 1,000 square feet of floor framing area?

    A. 4-5   B. 7-8   C. 8-10   D. 10-12

    2.___

3. What is represented by the electrical symbol shown at the right?

    A. Transformer   B. Buzzer
    C. Telephone   D. Bell

    3.___

4. Which of the following structures would typically require a relatively higher grade of lumber?

    A. Vertical stud   B. Joist
    C. Column   D. Mud sill

    4.___

5. A dump truck with a capacity of 10-12 cubic yards must load, drive, dump, and reposition itself over a 1-mile haul distance.
What average amount of time should be estimated for this sequence?

    A. 15 minutes   B. 30 minutes
    C. 1 hour   D. 2 hours

    5.___

6. The stripping of forms that are to be reused should be charged as

    A. common labor   B. masonry labor
    C. carpentry labor   D. material credit

    6.___

7. What type of brick masonry unit is represented by the drawing shown at the right?
    A. Modular
    B. Norwegian
    C. 3 core
    D. Economy

    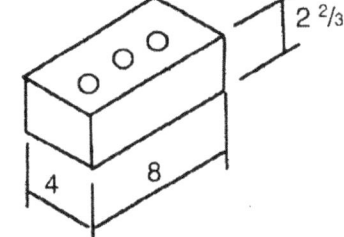

    7.___

8. Which of the following would be a typical thickness of a crushed-rock base course for an area of asphalt paving?

    A. 2"   B. 5"   C. 7"   D. 10"

    8.___

2 (#2)

9. Which of the following wood floor materials would be MOST expensive to install?

   A. Unfinished plank
   B. Walnut parquet
   C. Maple strip
   D. Oak parquet

10. When calculating the air-conditioning needs for a building, a loss factor of _____ should be used for the exposure of walls to common heated surfaces.

    A. 2.0
    B. 3.5
    C. 6.0
    D. 7.5

11. Approximately how many linear feet of moldings, door and window trim, handrails, or similar parts can a carpenter install in a typical work day?

    A. 100
    B. 250
    C. 400
    D. 500

12. Which of the following constructions is NOT typically found in bathroom lavatories?

    A. Enameled pressed steel
    B. Cast iron
    C. Cast ceramic
    D. Stainless steel

13. What size reinforcing bar is typically used for masonry walls?

    A. 3
    B. 4
    C. 7
    D. 9

14. Which of the following would NOT be a typical source for a cost-per-square-foot estimate?

    A. Architect
    B. Engineer
    C. Appraiser
    D. Building contractor

15. Approximately how many stair treads with risers can a carpenter install in an average work day?

    A. 5-8
    B. 10-12
    C. 15-18
    D. 21-25

16. Each of the following materials is commonly used as sheet metal flashing for roof waterproofing EXCEPT

    A. lead
    B. galvanized steel
    C. copper
    D. zinc

17. The MOST commonly used type of metal lath for wall support is

    A. self-furring
    B. flat rib
    C. flat diamond mesh
    D. 3/8" rib

18. Approximately how long will it take to install a non-mortised lockset?

    A. 15 minutes
    B. 30 minutes
    C. 1 hour
    D. 2 hours

19. What is represented by the architectural symbol shown at the right?

    A. Cut stone
    B. Concrete block
    C. Rubble stone
    D. Brick

20. What type of nails are typically used for installing floor sheathing?

    A. 4d
    B. 8d
    C. 12d
    D. 16d

21. Each of the following is considered *finish* electrical work EXCEPT

    A. outlet boxes
    B. light fixtures
    C. connection of fixtures to wiring
    D. switches

22. Which component of cost estimating typically presents the GREATEST difficulty?

    A. Materials
    B. Overhead
    C. Profit
    D. Labor

23. Approximately how many hours will it take to install and caulk a typical sliding shower door assembly?

    A. 2   B. 4   C. 6   D. 8

24. What is represented by the electrical symbol shown at the right?

    A. Single pole switch
    B. Lock or key switch
    C. Service weather head
    D. Main switch

25. Approximately how many exterior square feet can one painter cover, applying a primer coat and two coats of finish paint, in an average work day?

    A. 100   B. 250   C. 350   D. 500

KEY (CORRECT ANSWERS)

1.	D	11.	B
2.	B	12.	D
3.	C	13.	B
4.	B	14.	C
5.	B	15.	C
6.	C	16.	A
7.	A	17.	C
8.	B	18.	B
9.	B	19.	A
10.	B	20.	B

21. A
22. D
23. B
24. A
25. D

TEST 3

DIRECTIONS: Each question or incomplete statement is followed by several suggested answers or completions. Select the one that BEST answers the question or completes the statement. *PRINT THE LETTER OF THE CORRECT ANSWER IN THE SPACE AT THE RIGHT.*

1. Irregular shapes and narrow lites typically reduce the rate of glass installation by _____%.

    A. 10-20 B. 25-35 C. 30-50 D. 55-75

2. What is represented by the electrical symbol shown at the right?

    A. Exposed wiring B. Fusible element
    C. Three-way switch D. Circuit breaker

3. Approximately how many square feet of siding can be installed by a crew in a typical work day?

    A. 250 B. 500 C. 750 D. 1,000

4. What is the construction term for hinges used on doors?

    A. Gables B. Butts C. Hips D. Plates

5. Floor joists are typically spaced about _____ apart.

    A. 16" B. 2 feet C. 3 feet D. 4 feet

6. Which of the following paving materials is generally MOST expensive?

    A. Brick on sand bed B. Random flagstone
    C. Asphalt D. Concrete

7. Approximately how long should it take a 2-person crew to install floor joists for a 100 square-foot area of floor space?

    A. 30 minutes B. 1 hour
    C. 3 hours D. 1 work day

8. A _____ is represented by the mechanical symbol shown at the right.

    A. pressure-reducing valve B. motor-operated valve
    C. lock and shield valve D. globe valve

9. On average, labor costs for a job will be about _____% of the total job cost.

    A. 15 B. 35 C. 55 D. 85

10. Most exterior paint averages a coverage of about _____ square feet per gallon.

    A. 100 B. 250 C. 400 D. 550

11. What type of window includes two sashes which slide vertically?　　　　　11.___

    A. Double-hung　　　　　　　　　　B. Screen
    C. Casement　　　　　　　　　　　　D. Sliding

12. Approximately how many linear feet of drywall tape can be applied during an average　　12.___
    work day?

    A. 250　　　　　B. 400　　　　　C. 750　　　　　D. 1,000

13. What is used to join lengths of copper pipe?　　　　　13.___

    A. Molten solder
    B. Threaded ends and sealer
    C. Nipples
    D. Lead-and-oakum seal

14. Typically, one gallon of prepared wallpaper paste will supply adhesive for _____ full rolls　　14.___
    of wall covering.

    A. 8　　　　　B. 12　　　　　C. 24　　　　　D. 36

15. What is represented by the electrical symbol shown at the right?　　　　　15.___

    A. Range outlet
    B. Wall bracket light fixture
    C. Split-wired receptacle
    D. Special purpose outlet

16. What size is MOST wire used in residential work?　　　　　16.___

    A. 6　　　　　B. 8　　　　　C. 12　　　　　D. 16

17. Most fire codes require fire-resistant floor underneath fireplace units which extends to at　　17.___
    least _____ inches beyond the unit.

    A. 6　　　　　B. 12　　　　　C. 18　　　　　D. 24

18. If a building is constructed without a basement, _____ are typically used as footings.　　18.___

    A. joists　　　　　　　　　　　　　　B. staked caissons
    C. grade beams　　　　　　　　　　D. mud sills

19. What is the MOST commonly used size range for flashing and gutter sheet metal?　　19.___

    A. 8-12　　　　　B. 14-18　　　　　C. 22-26　　　　　D. 24-30

20. Approximately how many square feet of interior wall space can one painter, using a　　20.___
    brush, cover in an hour?

    A. 25-50　　　　　B. 100　　　　　C. 175-200　　　　　D. 250

21. Which of the following downspout materials would be MOST expensive?　　　　　21.___

    A. Copper　　　　　　　　　　　　　B. Aluminum
    C. Zinc　　　　　　　　　　　　　　D. Stainless steel

22. What is represented by the mechanical symbol shown at the right?   22._____

    A. Expansion valve   B. Floor drain
    C. Shower   D. Scale trap

23. Approximately how much lead (pounds) is required per joint in one sewer line lead-and-   23._____
    oakum seal?

    A. 1/4   B. 1/2   C. 1 1/2   D. 3

24. Which of the following caulking materials is MOST expensive?   24._____

    A. Neoprene   B. Butyl
    C. Polyurethane   D. Latex

25. The assembly inside a tank toilet that controls the water supply is the   25._____

    A. P trap   B. bell-and-spigot
    C. gating   D. ball cock

KEY (CORRECT ANSWERS)

1.	C	11.	A
2.	B	12.	A
3.	A	13.	A
4.	B	14.	B
5.	A	15.	C
6.	D	16.	C
7.	C	17.	B
8.	D	18.	C
9.	A	19.	C
10.	C	20.	B

21. A
22. A
23. A
24. B
25. C

SAFETY
EXAMINATION SECTION
TEST 1

DIRECTIONS: Each question or incomplete statement is followed by several suggested answers or completions. Select the one that BEST answers the question or completes the statement. *PRINT THE LETTER OF THE CORRECT ANSWER IN THE SPACE AT THE RIGHT.*

1. Which one of the following is an INCORRECT safety guideline? 1.____

   A. All working conditions and equipment should be considered carefully before beginning an operation.
   B. Aisles should be lighted properly.
   C. Personnel should be provided with protective clothing essential to safe performance of a task.
   D. In manual lifting, the worker must keep his knees straight and lift with the arm muscles.

2. Of the following, the supply item with the GREATEST susceptibility to spontaneous heating is 2.____

   A. alcohol, ethyl   B. kerosene
   C. candles   D. turpentine

Questions 3-7.

DIRECTIONS: Questions 3 through 7 are descriptions of accidents that occurred in a warehouse. For each accident, choose the letter in front of the safety measure that is MOST likely to prevent a repetition of the accident indicated.

SAFETY MEASURE

   A. Posting warning signs
   B. Redesign of layout or facilities
   C. Repairing, improving or replacing supplies, tools or equipment
   D. Training the staff in safe practices

3. After a new all-glass door was installed at the entrance to the warehouse, one of the employees banged his head into the door causing a large lump on his forehead when he failed to realize that the door was closed. 3.____

4. While tieing up a package with manila rope, an employee got several small rope splinters in his right hand and he had to have medical treatment to remove the splinters. 4.____

5. An employee discovered a small fire in a wastepaper basket but was unable to prevent it from spreading because all the nearby fire extinguishers were inaccessible due to skids of material being stacked in front of the extinguishers. 5.____

6. When a laborer attempted to drop the tailgate of a delivery truck while the truck was being backed into the loading dock, he had his fingers crushed when the truck continued to move while he was working on lowering the tailgate. 6.____

7. An employee carrying a carton with both hands tripped over a broom which had been left lying in an aisle by another employee after the latter had swept the aisle.

7.___

8. Safety experts agree that accidents can probably BEST be prevented by

8.___

   A. developing safety consciousness among employees
   B. developing a program which publicizes major accidents
   C. penalizing employees the first time they do not follow safety procedures
   D. giving recognition to employees with accident-free records

9. The accident records of many agencies indicate that most on-the-job injuries are caused by the unsafe acts of their employees.
Which one of the following statements pinpoints the MOST probable cause of this safety problem?

9.___

   A. Responsibility for preventing on-the-job accidents has not been delegated.
   B. Lack of proper supervision has permitted these unsafe actions to continue.
   C. No consideration has been given to eliminating environmental job hazards.
   D. Penalties for causing on-the-job accidents are not sufficiently severe.

10. Which of the following methods is LEAST essential to the success of an accident prevention program?

10.___

   A. Determining corrective measures by analyzing the causes of accidents and making recommendations to eliminate them
   B. Educating employees as to the importance of safe working conditions and methods
   C. Determining accident causes by seeking out the conditions from which each accident has developed
   D. Holding each supervisor responsible for accidents occurring during the on-the-job performance of his immediate subordinates

11. The effectiveness of a public relations program in a public agency is BEST indicated by the

11.___

   A. amount of mass media publicity favorable to the policies of the agency
   B. morale of those employees who directly serve the patrons of the agency
   C. public's understanding and support of the agency's program and policies
   D. number of complaints received by the agency from patrons using its facilities

12. Buttered bread and coffee dropped on an office floor in a terminal are

12.___

   A. minor hazards which should cause no serious injury
   B. unattractive, but not dangerous
   C. the most dangerous types of office hazards
   D. hazards which should be corrected immediately

13. A laborer was sent upstairs to get a 20-pound sack of rock salt. While going downstairs and reading the printing on the sack, he fell, and the sack of rock salt fell and broke his toe.
Which of the following is MOST likely to have been the MOST important cause of the accident?
The

13.___

A. stairs were beginning to become worn
B. laborer was carrying too heavy a sack of rock salt
C. rock salt was in a place that was too inaccessible
D. laborer was not careful about the way he went down the stairs

14. A COMMONLY recommended safe distance between the foot of an extension ladder and the wall against which it is placed is

    A. 3 feet for ladders less than 18 feet in height
    B. between 3 feet and 6 feet for ladders less than 18 feet in length
    C. 1/8 the length of the extended ladder
    D. 1/4 the length of the extended ladder

15. The BEST type of fire extinguisher for electrical fires is the _____ extinguisher.

    A. dry chemical   B. foam
    C. carbon monoxide   D. baking soda-acid

16. A Class A extinguisher should be used for fires in

    A. potassium, magnesium, zinc, sodium
    B. electrical wiring
    C. oil, gasoline
    D. wood, paper, and textiles

17. The one of the following which is NOT a safe practice when lifting heavy objects is:

    A. Keep the back as nearly upright as possible
    B. If the object feels too heavy, keep lifting until you get help
    C. Spread the feet apart
    D. Use the arm and leg muscles

18. In a shop, it would be MOST necessary to provide a fitted cover on the metal container for

    A. old paint brushes   B. oily rags and waste
    C. sand   D. broken glass

19. Safety shoes usually have the unique feature of

    A. extra hard heels and soles to prevent nails from piercing the shoes
    B. special leather to prevent the piercing of the shoes by falling objects
    C. a metal guard over the toes which is built into the shoes
    D. a non-slip tread on the heels and soles

20. Of the following, the MOST important factor contributing to a helper's safety on the job is for him to

    A. work slowly   B. wear gloves
    C. be alert   D. know his job well

21. If it is necessary for you to lift one end of a piece of heavy equipment with a crowbar in order to allow a maintainer to work underneath it, the BEST of the following procedures to follow is to

   A. support the handle of the bar on a box
   B. insert temporary blocks to support the piece
   C. call the supervisor to help you
   D. wear heavy gloves

22. Of the following, the MOST important reason for not letting oily rags accumulate in an open storage bin is that they

   A. may start a fire by spontaneous combustion
   B. will drip oil onto other items in the bin
   C. may cause a foul odor
   D. will make the area messy

23. Of the following, the BEST method to employ in putting out a gasoline fire is to

   A. use a bucket of water
   B. smother it with rags
   C. use a carbon dioxide extinguisher
   D. use a carbon tetrachloride extinguisher

24. When opening an emergency exit door set in the sidewalk, the door should be raised slowly to avoid

   A. a sudden rush of air from the street
   B. making unnecessary noise
   C. damage to the sidewalk
   D. injuring pedestrians

25. The BEST reason to turn off lights when cleaning lampshades on electrical fixtures is to

   A. conserve energy
   B. avoid electrical shock
   C. prevent breakage of lightbulbs
   D. prevent unnecessary eye strain

KEY (CORRECT ANSWERS)

1. D
2. D
3. A
4. D
5. B

6. D
7. D
8. A
9. B
10. D

11. C
12. D
13. D
14. D
15. A

16. D
17. B
18. B
19. C
20. C

21. B
22. A
23. C
24. D
25. B

TEST 2

DIRECTIONS: Each question or incomplete statement is followed by several suggested answers or completions. Select the one that BEST answers the question or completes the statement. *PRINT THE LETTER OF THE CORRECT ANSWER IN THE SPACE AT THE RIGHT.*

1. The MOST important reason for roping off a work area in a terminal is to   1.___

    A. protect the public
    B. protect the repair crew
    C. prevent distraction of the crew by the public
    D. prevent delays to the public

2. Shoes which have a sponge rubber sole should NOT be worn around a work area because such a sole   2.___

    A. will wear quickly
    B. is not waterproof
    C. does not keep the feet warm
    D. is easily punctured by steel objects

3. When repair work is being done on an elevated structure, canvas spreads are suspended under the working area MAINLY to   3.___

    A. reduce noise
    B. discourage crowds
    C. protect the structure
    D. protect pedestrians

4. It is poor practice to hold a piece of wood in the hands or lap when tightening a screw in the wood.
    This is for the reason that   4.___

    A. sufficient leverage cannot be obtained
    B. the screwdriver may bend
    C. the wood will probably split
    D. personal injury is likely to result

5. Steel helmets give workers the MOST protection from   5.___

    A. falling objects
    B. eye injuries
    C. fire
    D. electric shock

6. It is POOR practice to wear goggles   6.___

    A. when chipping stone
    B. when using a grinder
    C. while climbing or descending ladders
    D. when handling molten metal

7. When using a brace and bit to bore a hole completely through a partition, it is MOST important to   7.___

A. lean heavily on the brace and bit
B. maintain a steady turning speed all through the job
C. have the body in a position that will not be easily thrown off balance
D. reverse the direction of the bit at frequent intervals

8. Gloves should be used when handling   8._____

  A. lanterns   B. wooden rules
  C. heavy ropes   D. all small tools

Questions 9-16.

DIRECTIONS: Questions 9 through 16, inclusive, are based on the ladder safety rules given below. Read these rules fully before answering these items.

LADDER SAFETY RULES

When a ladder is placed on a slightly uneven supporting surface, use a flat piece of board or small wedge to even up the ladder feet. To secure the proper angle for resting a ladder, it should be placed so that the distance from the base of the ladder to the supporting wall is 1/4 the length of the ladder. To avoid overloading a ladder, only one person should work on a ladder at a time. Do not place a ladder in front of a door. When the top rung of a ladder rests against a pole, the ladder should be lashed securely. Clear loose stones or debris from the ground around the base of a ladder before climbing. While on a ladder, do not attempt to lean so that any part of the body, except arms or hands, extends more than 12 inches beyond the side rail. Always face the ladder when ascending or descending. When carrying ladders through buildings, watch for ceiling globes and lighting fixtures. Avoid the use of rolling ladders as scaffold supports.

9. A small wedge is used to   9._____

  A. even up the feet of a ladder resting on an uneven surface
  B. lock the wheels of a roller ladder
  C. secure the proper resting angle for a ladder
  D. secure a ladder against a pole

10. An 8 foot ladder resting against a wall should be so inclined that the distance between the base of the ladder and the wall is _____ feet.   10._____

  A. 2   B. 5   C. 7   D. 9

11. A ladder should be lashed securely when   11._____

  A. it is placed in front of a door
  B. loose stones are on the ground near the base of the ladder
  C. the top rung rests against a pole
  D. two people are working from the same ladder

12. Rolling ladders   12._____

  A. should be used for scaffold supports
  B. should not be used for scaffold supports
  C. are useful on uneven ground
  D. should be used against a pole

13. When carrying a ladder through a building, it is necessary to

    A. have two men to carry it
    B. carry the ladder vertically
    C. watch for ceiling globes
    D. face the ladder while carrying it

14. It is POOR practice to

    A. lash a ladder securely at any time
    B. clear debris from the base of a ladder before climbing
    C. even up the feet of a ladder resting on slightly uneven ground
    D. place a ladder in front of a door

15. A person on a ladder should NOT extend his head beyond the side rail by more than_____ inches.

    A. 12 B. 9 C. 7 D. 5

16. The MOST important reason for permitting only one person to work on a ladder at a time is that

    A. both could not face the ladder at one time
    B. the ladder will be overloaded
    C. time would be lost going up and down the ladder
    D. they would obstruct each other

17. Many portable electric power tools, such as electric drills, have a third conductor in the power lead which is used to connect the case of the tool to a grounded part of the electric outlet.
    The reason for this extra conductor is to

    A. have a spare wire in case one power wire should break
    B. strengthen the power lead so it cannot easily be damaged
    C. prevent the user of the tool from being shocked
    D. enable the tool to be used for long periods of time without overheating

18. Protective goggles should NOT be worn when

    A. standing on a ladder drilling a steel beam
    B. descending a ladder after completing a job
    C. chipping concrete near a third rail
    D. sharpening a cold chisel on a grinding stone

19. When the foot of an extension ladder, placed against a high wall, rests on a sidewalk or another such similar surface, it is advisable to tie a rope between the bottom rung of the ladder and a point on the wall opposite this rung.
    This is done to prevent

    A. people from walking under the ladder
    B. another worker from removing the ladder
    C. the ladder from vibrating when ascending or descending
    D. the foot of the ladder from slipping

20. In construction work, practically all accidents can be blamed on the   20.____
    A. failure of an individual to give close attention to the job assigned to him
    B. use of improper tools
    C. lack of cooperation among the men in a gang
    D. fact that an incompetent man was placed in a key position

21. If it is necessary for you to do some work with your hands under a piece of heavy equip-   21.____
    ment while a fellow worker lifts up and holds one end of it by means of a pinch bar, one
    important precaution you should take is to

    A. wear gloves
    B. watch the bar to be ready if it slips
    C. insert a temporary block to support the piece
    D. work as fast as possible

22. Employees of the transit system whose work requires them to enter upon the tracks in   22.____
    the subway are cautioned not to wear loose fitting clothing.
    The MOST important reason for this caution is that loose fitting clothing may

    A. interfere when men are using heavy tools
    B. catch on some projection of a passing train
    C. tear more easily than snug fitting clothing
    D. give insufficient protection against subway dust

23. The MOST important reason for insisting on neatness in maintenance quarters is that it   23.____

    A. keeps the men busy in slack periods
    B. prevents tools from becoming rusty
    C. makes a good impression on visitors and officials
    D. decreases the chances of accidents to employees

24. Maintenance workers whose duties require them to do certain types of work generally   24.____
    work in pairs.
    The LEAST likely of the following possible reasons for this practice is that

    A. some of the work requires two men
    B. the men can help each other in case of accident
    C. there is too much equipment for one man to carry
    D. it protects against vandalism

25. A foreman reprimands a helper for actions in violation of the rules and regulations.   25.____
    The BEST reaction of the helper in this situation is to

    A. tell the foreman that he was careful and that he did not take any chances
    B. explain that he took this action to save time
    C. keep quiet and accept the criticism
    D. demand that the foreman show him the rule he violated

KEY (CORRECT ANSWERS)

1.	A	11.	C
2.	D	12.	B
3.	D	13.	C
4.	D	14.	D
5.	A	15.	A
6.	C	16.	B
7.	C	17.	C
8.	C	18.	B
9.	A	19.	D
10.	A	20.	A

21. C
22. B
23. D
24. D
25. C

EXAMINATION SECTION
TEST 1

DIRECTIONS: Each question or incomplete statement is followed by several suggested answers or completions. Select the one that BEST answers the question or completes the statement. *PRINT THE LETTER OF THE CORRECT ANSWER IN THE SPACE AT THE RIGHT.*

1. Which of the following devices has the HIGHEST energy efficiency?   1.____

   A. Diesel engine
   B. Small electric motor
   C. Home gas furnace
   D. Solar cell

2. A change in the quality of an environment, caused by an increase in temperature, is called   2.____

   A. thermal pollution
   B. oxidation
   C. thermodynamics
   D. transpiration

3. Which of the following industries places the HIGHEST energy demands on the environment?   3.____

   A. Food production and processing
   B. Paper and related products
   C. Stone, clay, glass, and concrete production
   D. Chemicals and chemical products

4. The environmental influence responsible for more human illness than any other factor is   4.____

   A. nuclear waste
   B. air pollution
   C. acid rain
   D. water pollution

5. Which of the following is NOT a difficulty involved in putting wind energy to use?   5.____

   A. Harnessing the three-dimensional dispersion of wind
   B. Finding locations that are consistently windy enough to be useful
   C. Erratic and variable speeds of most winds
   D. Inefficient transmission of energy from collection sites to populations

6. Which of the following classes of insecticides will break down MOST quickly after their use?   6.____

   A. Chlorinated hydrocarbons, such as DDT
   B. Botanicals, such as Rotenone
   C. Organophosphates, such as Malathion
   D. Carbamates, such as Sevin

7. In harvesting coal from the earth, the difference between tunnel and strip mining is that strip mining   7.____

   A. is more expensive
   B. is less efficient
   C. is more likely to cause soil erosion
   D. disrupts the flow of ground water

8. The MAIN portion of metallic lead toxins are produced by

   A. paint products
   B. automobile emissions
   C. commercial pesticides
   D. home electricity

9. What is the common name for a heat pump that heats the exterior at the expense of the interior?

   A. Furnace
   B. Generator
   C. Refrigerator
   D. Turbine

10. Artificially raising the temperature of aquatic environments has a negative effect on aquatic organisms because

    A. some organisms become infertile at warmer temperatures
    B. warm water carries less oxygen than cold
    C. the mobility of larger organisms is decreased
    D. warm water interferes with the photosynthesis of microorganisms

11. The type of energy source that does NOT add additional heat to the environment is

    A. solar
    B. fossil fuel
    C. hydroelectric
    D. tidal

12. Which of the following is NOT a drawback involved with the use of agricultural insecticides?

    A. Gradual acquisition of immunity by pest populations
    B. The loss of beneficial insects, such as wasps
    C. Eventual damage to plant matter in crops
    D. Environmental contamination from chemical residues

13. Radiation that arises from natural radioactive materials that are ALWAYS present in the environment is called

    A. background radiation
    B. ionizing radiation
    C. backfill
    D. alpha radiation

14. The INITIAL factor in the formation of natural oil and gas deposits is

    A. large accumulations of organic matter
    B. seismic activity beneath the earth"s surface
    C. drying-out of large bodies of water
    D. volcanic mixture of earthly minerals

15. What is the APPROXIMATE percentage of air pollutants, by weight, that come directly from automobiles?

    A. 10%   B. 40%   C. 65%   D. 80%

16. In detergents, the additives that extract minerals from washing water are

    A. enzymes
    B. lyes
    C. phosphates
    D. nitrates

17. Which of the following methods of transportation requires the LOWEST expense of energy per person/passenger?

   A. Walking
   B. Train
   C. Intercity bus
   D. Bicycle

18. Which of the following chemical compounds is a component of acid rain?

   A. Hydrogen sulfide
   B. Carbon monoxide
   C. Hydrocarbon
   D. Sulfur dioxide

19. Most of the electricity used in the United States today is generated by

   A. solar cells
   B. tidal generators
   C. steam turbines
   D. internal combustion engines

20. Which of the following methods of municipal waste is MOST harmful to the environment and surrounding populations?

   A. Open dumping
   B. Sanitary landfill
   C. Incineration
   D. Incineration and ocean dumping

21. Which of the following is NOT a problem posed by the construction of hydroelectric dams?

   A. Wildlife habitat destruction
   B. Water loss through evaporation
   C. Total obstruction of seasonal water flow
   D. Silting-up of reservoirs

22. Each of the following is a principal constituent of fertilizer runoff EXCEPT

   A. hydrocarbons
   B. nitrates
   C. potash
   D. phosphates

23. Of the following, which industry is responsible for the GREATEST amount of hazardous wastes imposed upon the environment?

   A. Organic chemicals, pesticides, and explosives
   B. Pharmaceuticals
   C. Petroleum refining
   D. Smelting and refining of primary metals

24. Which of the following is a non-renewable energy resource?

   A. Tidal currents
   B. Natural oil/gas deposits
   C. Solar heat
   D. Geothermal energy

25. The suspension of air pollutants in the atmosphere near the earth's surface is caused by

   A. littoral drift
   B. convection
   C. thermal inversion
   D. acid rain

KEY (CORRECT ANSWERS)

1.	C	11.	A
2.	A	12.	C
3.	D	13.	A
4.	D	14.	A
5.	B	15.	B
6.	B	16.	C
7.	C	17.	D
8.	B	18.	D
9.	C	19.	C
10.	B	20.	A

21. C
22. A
23. A
24. B
25. C

TEST 2

DIRECTIONS: Each question or incomplete statement is followed by several suggested answers or completions. Select the one that BEST answers the question or completes the statement. *PRINT THE LETTER OF THE CORRECT ANSWER IN THE SPACE AT THE RIGHT.*

1. Which of the following sources is responsible for the GREATEST level of ozone depletion in the earth's atmosphere? 1.____

    A. Aerosol propellants
    B. Commercial and residential refrigeration
    C. Production of plastic foam and insulation
    D. Solvent cleaning of metal and electronic parts

2. High concentrations of mercury and aluminum in soil are caused by 2.____

    A. acid contamination   B. plant respiration
    C. ammonia seepage   D. natural decomposition

3. Which of the following waste products is MOST abundant in landfill sites? 3.____

    A. Paper products   B. Plastics
    C. Glass   D. Metals

4. Which of the following types of cells are LEAST susceptible to contamination from nuclear waste? 4.____

    A. Reproductive   B. Blood
    C. Lymph   D. Nerve

5. Which of the following effects is caused by the runoff of agricultural fertilizers into surface water supplies? 5.____

    A. Sterilization of larger aquatic vertebrates
    B. Killing algae and other microorganisms
    C. Increasing mercury content
    D. Eventual depletion of oxygen

6. Traditionally, most low-level nuclear wastes produced in the United States have been disposed of 6.____

    A. in deep formations of stable rock
    B. under sheets of polar ice
    C. in shallow land-burial sites
    D. far into the open sea

7. Which of the following is the result of atmospheric decomposition that comes from emissions of sulfur dioxide and oxides of nitrogen? 7.____

    A. Ozone depletion   B. Smog
    C. Fermentation   D. Acid rain

83

8. Highly toxic chemicals, such as PCBs, that are the byproducts of manufacturing processes or waste-burning are called

   A. hydrocarbons
   B. solvents
   C. dioxins
   D. fluorocarbons

9. Which of the following is NOT a potential source of fossil fuel?

   A. Iron ore
   B. Tar sand
   C. Shale
   D. Underground methane

10. Each of the following is considered an effective material for lining the disposal sites of toxic wastes EXCEPT

    A. clay
    B. rubber
    C. plastic
    D. sandstone

11. Which energy source presents the GREATEST risk to workers involved in the entire process of energy production?

    A. Coal
    B. Oil
    C. Natural gas
    D. Uranium

12. Water vapor that has collected around microscopic particles of air pollution is described as

    A. smog
    B. acid rain
    C. haze
    D. particulate

13. The PRIMARY stage of municipal sewage treatment removes which of the following elements from sewage?

    A. Dissolved chemicals
    B. Grit and coarse solids
    C. Sediments
    D. Microorganisms

14. Introducing microbes that feed on water contaminants into a polluted body of water is an example of

    A. adsorption
    B. bioremediation
    C. desalinization
    D. integrated pest control

15. Producing energy by splitting the nucleus of a single radioactive atom is called

    A. radiation
    B. nuclear fission
    C. neutron chain reaction
    D. nuclear fusion

16. Which of the following is NOT a source of acid precipitation?

    A. Automobile emissions
    B. Nuclear power generation
    C. Coal-burning stoves
    D. Electrical plants powered by steam turbines

17. Currently, the LEAST plentiful energy source available to the United States from our natural reserves is

    A. petroleum
    B. natural gas
    C. coal
    D. uranium oxide

18. Which of the following chemical compounds is a PRIMARY cause of ozone depletion? 18._____

    A. Nitrogen oxide   B. Bicarbonate
    C. Dioxin   D. Chlorofluorocarbon

19. Which of the following is a function performed by a solar collector? 19._____

    A. Heating water
    B. Using sunlight to ignite combustible materials
    C. Converting sunlight to electricity
    D. Storing energy

20. Sulfur dioxide, a poisonous gas, is produced by the 20._____

    A. use of aerosol sprays
    B. evaporation of acid-contaminated waters
    C. burning of coal
    D. upwelling of poorly-contained nuclear wastes

21. Which of the following is an example of *point source* water pollution? 21._____

    A. Agricultural runoff into streams
    B. Seepage of industrial chemicals into groundwater supplies
    C. An oil spill caused by the wreck of a tanker
    D. Acid rain contamination of a large lake

22. Which non-chemical pollutant has proven MOST hazardous to marine and aquatic wildlife? 22._____

    A. Metals   B. Paper products
    C. Plastics   D. Construction by-products

23. Most of the thermoplastics produced in the United States are from which of the following categories? 23._____

    A. Polyethylene   B. Polystyrene
    C. Polypropylene   D. Polyurethane

24. Each of the following is an example of a *soft* energy resource EXCEPT 24._____

    A. geothermal heat   B. wind energy
    C. natural gas deposits   D. solar power

25. Which type of coal has the GREATEST heating potential? 25._____

    A. Bituminous   B. Anthracite
    C. Subbituminous   D. Lignite

KEY (CORRECT ANSWERS)

1.	C	11.	A
2.	A	12.	C
3.	A	13.	B
4.	D	14.	B
5.	D	15.	B
6.	C	16.	B
7.	D	17.	A
8.	C	18.	D
9.	A	19.	A
10.	D	20.	C

21. C
22. C
23. A
24. C
25. B

EXAMINATION SECTION
TEST 1

DIRECTIONS: Each question or incomplete statement is followed by several suggested answers or completions. Select the one that BEST answers the question or completes the statement. *PRINT THE LETTER OF THE CORRECT ANSWER IN THE SPACE AT THE RIGHT.*

1. At times there may be a conflict between employees' needs and agency goals. A supervisor's MAIN role in motivating employees in such circumstances is to try to
   A. develop good work habits among the employees whom he supervises
   B. emphasize the importance of material rewards such as merit increases
   C. keep careful records of employees' performance for possible disciplinary action
   D. reconcile employees' objectives with those of the public agency

2. Organizations cannot function effectively without policies.
   However, when an organization imposes excessively detailed policy restrictions, it is MOST likely to lead to
   A. conflicts among individual employees
   B. a lack of adequate supervision
   C. a reduction of employee initiative
   D. a reliance on punitive discipline

3. The PRIMARY responsibility for establishing good employee relations in the public service usually rests with
   A. employees   B. management
   C. civil service organizations   D. employee organizations

4. At times, certain off-the-job conduct of public employees may be of concern to management. This concern stems from the fact that
   A. agency programs could be harmed by adverse publicity if employees' conduct is considered detrimental by the public
   B. fairness to all concerned is usually the major consideration in disciplinary cases
   C. public employees must meet higher standards than employees working in private industry
   D. public employees have high ethical standards and may participate in social action programs

5. At one time or another, most employees ask for, or expect, special treatment. For a supervisor faced with this problem, the one of the following which is the MOST valid guideline is:
   A. According to the rules, a supervisor must give identical treatment to all his subordinates, regardless of the circumstances.

B. Although all employees have equal rights, it is sometimes necessary to give an employee special treatment to meet an individual need.
C. It would damage morale if any employee were to receive special treatment, regardless of circumstances.
D. Since each employee has different needs, there is little reason to maintain general rules.

6. Mental health problems exist in many parts of our society and may also be found in the work setting.
The BASIC role of the supervisor in relation to the mental health problems of his subordinates is to
    A. restrict himself solely to the taking of disciplinary measures, if warranted, and follow up carefully
    B. avoid involvement in personal matters
    C. identify mental health problems as early as possible
    D. resolve mental health problems through personal counseling

6._____

7. Supervisory expectation of high levels of employee performance, where such performance is possible, is MOST likely to lead to employees'
    A. expecting frequent praise and encouragement
    B. gaining a greater sense of satisfaction
    C. needing less detailed instructions than previously
    D. reducing their quantitative output

7._____

8. In public agencies, as elsewhere, supervisors sometimes compete with one another to increase their units' productivity.
Of the following, the MAJOR disadvantage of such competition, from the general viewpoint of providing good public service, is that
    A. while individual employee effort will increase, unit productivity will decrease
    B. employees will be discouraged from sincere interest in their work
    C. the supervisors' competition may hinder the achievement of agency goals
    D. total payroll costs will increase as the activities of each unit increase

8._____

9. If employees are motivated primarily by material compensation, the amount of effort an individual employee will put into performing his work effectively will depend MAINLY upon how he perceives
    A. cooperation to be tied to successful effort
    B. the association between good work and increased compensation
    C. the public status of his particular position
    D. the supervisor's behavior in work situations

9._____

10. Cash awards to individual employees are sometimes used to encourage useful suggestions. However, some management experts believe that awards should involve some form of employee recognition other than cash.
Which of the following reasons BEST supports opposition to using cash as a reward for worthwhile suggestions?

10._____

A. Cash awards cause employees to expend excessive time in making suggestions.
B. Taxpayer opposition to dash awards has increased following generous salary increases for public employees in recent years.
C. Public funds expended on awards leads to a poor image of public employees.
D. The use of cash awards raises the problem of deciding the monetary value of suggestions.

11. The BEST general rule for a supervisor to follow in giving praise and criticism is to
    A. criticize and praise publicly
    B. criticize publicly and praise privately
    C. praise and criticize privately
    D. praise publicly and criticize privately

12. An important step in designing an error-control policy is to determine the maximum number of errors that can be considered acceptable for the entire organization.
    Of the following, the MOST important factor in making such a decision is the
    A. number of clerical staff available to check for errors
    B. frequency of errors by supervisors
    C. human and material costs of errors
    D. number of errors that will become known to the public

13. When a supervisor tries to correct a situation where errors have been widespread, he should concentrate his efforts, and those of the employees involved, on
    A. avoiding future mistakes   B. fixing appropriate blame
    C. preparing a written report   D. determining fair penalties

14. When delegating work to a subordinate, a supervisor should ALWAYS tell the subordinate
    A. each step in the procedure for doing the work
    B. how much time to expend
    C. what is to be accomplished
    D. whether reports are necessary

15. The responsibilities of all employees should be clearly defined and understood. In addition, in order for employees to successfully fulfill their responsibilities, they should also GENERALLY be given
    A. written directives   B. close supervision
    C. corresponding authority   D. daily instructions

16. The one of the following types of training in which positive transfer of training to the actual work situation is MOST likely to take place is _____ training.
    A. conference   B. demonstration
    C. classroom   D. on-the-job

17. The type of training or instruction in which the subject matter is presented in small units called frames is known as
    A. programmed instruction
    B. reinforcement
    C. remediation
    D. skills training

18. In order to bring about maximum learning in a training situation, a supervisor acting as a trainer should attempt to create a setting in which
    A. all trainees experience a large amount of failure as an incentive
    B. all trainees experience a small amount of failure as an incentive
    C. each trainee experiences approximately the same amounts of success and failure
    D. each trainee experiences as much success and as little failure as possible

19. Assume that, in a training course given by an agency, the instructor conducts a brief quiz, on paper, toward the close of each session.
    From the point of view of maximizing learning, it would be BEST for the instructor to
    A. wait until the last session to provide the correct answers
    B. give the correct answers aloud immediately after each quiz
    C. permit trainees to take the questions home with them so that they can look up the answers
    D. wait until the next session to provide the correct answers

20. A supervisor, in the course of evaluating employees, should ALWAYS determine whether
    A. employees realize that their work is under scrutiny
    B. the ratings will be included in permanent records
    C. employees meet standards of performance
    D. his statements on the rating form are similar to those made by the previous supervisor

21. All of the following are legitimate objectives of employee performance reporting systems EXCEPT
    A. serving as a check on personnel policies such as job qualification requirements and placement techniques
    B. determining who is the least efficient worker among a large number of employees
    C. improving employee performance by identifying strong and weak points in individual performance
    D. developing standards of satisfactory performance

22. Studies of existing employee performance evaluation schemes have revealed a common tendency to construct guides in order to measure <u>inferred</u> traits.
    Of the following, the BEST example of an inferred trait is
    A. appearance B. loyalty C. accuracy D. promptness

23. Which of the following is MOST likely to be a positive influence in promoting common agreement at a staff conference?
    A. A mature, tolerant group of participants
    B. A strong chairman with firm opinions
    C. The normal differences of human personalities
    D. The urge to forcefully support one's views

24. Before holding a problem-solving conference, the conference leader sent to each invitee an announcement on which he listed the names of all invitees. His action in listing the names was
    A. *wise*, mainly because all invitees will know who has been invited, and can, if necessary, plan a proper approach
    B. *unwise*, mainly because certain invitees could form factions prior to the conference
    C. *unwise*, mainly because invitees might come to the conference in a belligerent mood if they had had interpersonal conflicts with other invitees
    D. *wise*, mainly because invitees who are antagonistic to each other could decide not to attend

25. Methods analysis is a detailed study of existing or proposed work methods for the purpose of improving agency operations.
    Of the following, it is MOST accurate to say that this type of study
    A. can sometimes be made informally by the experienced supervisor who can identify problems and suggest solutions
    B. is not suitable for studying the operations of a public agency
    C. will be successfully accomplished only if an outside organization reviews agency operations
    D. usually costs more to complete than is justified by the potential economies to be realized

KEY (CORRECT ANSWERS)

1.	D		11.	D
2.	C		12.	C
3.	B		13.	A
4.	A		14.	C
5.	B		15.	C
6.	C		16.	D
7.	B		17.	A
8.	C		18.	D
9.	B		19.	B
10.	D		20.	C

21.
22. B
23. A
24. A
25. A

TEST 2

DIRECTIONS: Each question or incomplete statement is followed by several suggested answers or completions. Select the one that BEST answers the question or completes the statement. *PRINT THE LETTER OF THE CORRECT ANSWER IN THE SPACE AT THE RIGHT.*

1. Present-day managerial practices advocate that adequate hierarchical levels of communication be maintained among all levels of management.
   Of the following, the BEST way to accomplish this is with
   A. intradepartmental memoranda only
   B. interdepartmental memoranda only
   C. periodic staff meetings, interdepartmental and intradepartmental memoranda
   D. interdepartmental and intradepartmental memoranda

   1._____

2. It is generally agreed upon that it is important to have effective communications in the unit so that everyone knows exactly what is expected of him.
   Of the following, the communications system which can assist in fulfilling this objective BEST is one which consists of
   A. written policies and procedures for administrative functions and verbal policies and procedures for professional functions
   B. written policies and procedures for professional and administrative functions
   C. verbal policies and procedures for professional and administrative functions
   D. verbal policies and procedures for professional functions

   2._____

3. If a department manager wishes to build an effective department, he MOST generally must
   A. be able to hire and fire as he feels necessary
   B. consider the total aspects of his job, his influence and the effects of his decisions
   C. have access to reasonable amounts of personnel and money with which to build his programs
   D. attend as many professional conferences as possible so that he can keep up-to-date with all the latest advances in the field

   3._____

4. Of the following, the factor which generally contributes MOST effectively to the performance of the unit is that the supervisor
   A. personally inspect the work of all employees
   B. fill orders at a faster rate than his subordinates
   C. have an exact knowledge of theory
   D. implement a program of professional development for his staff

   4._____

5. Administrative policies relate MOST closely to
   A. control of commodities and personnel
   B. general policies emanating from the central office
   C. fiscal management of the department only
   D. handling and dispensing of funds

   5._____

6. Part of being a good supervisor is to be able to develop an attitude towards employees which will motivate them to do their best on the job.
   The GOOD supervisor, therefore, should
   A. take an interest in subordinates, but not develop an all-consuming attitude in this area
   B. remain in an aloof position when dealing with employees
   C. be as close to subordinates as possible on the job
   D. take a complete interest in all the activities of subordinates, both on and off the job

7. The practice of a supervisor assigning an experienced employee to train new employees instead of training them himself is GENERALLY considered
   A. *undesirable*; the more experienced employee will resent being taken away from his regular job
   B. *desirable*; the supervisor can then devote more time to his regular duties
   C. *undesirable*; the more experienced employee is not working at the proper level to train new employees
   D. *desirable*; the more experienced employee is probably a better trainer than the supervisor

8. It is generally agreed that on-the-job training is MOST effective when new employees are
   A. provided with study manuals, standard operating procedures and other written materials to be studied for at least two weeks before the employees attempt to do the job
   B. shown how to do the job in detail, and then instructed to do the work under close supervision
   C. trained by an experienced worker for at least a week to make certain that the employees can do the job
   D. given work immediately which is checked at the end of each day

9. Employees sometimes form small informal groups, commonly called cliques. With regard to the effect of such groups on processing of the workload, the attitude a supervisor should take towards these cliques is that of
   A. *acceptance*, since they take the employees' minds off their work without wasting too much time
   B. *rejection*, since those workers inside the clique tend to do less work than the outsiders
   C. *acceptance*, since the supervisor is usually included in the clique
   D. *rejection*, since they are usually disliked by higher management

10. Of the following, the BEST statement regarding rules and regulations in a unit is that they
    A. are "necessary evils" to be tolerated by those at and above the first supervisory level only
    B. are stated in broad, indefinite terms so as to allow maximum amount of leeway in complying with them

3 (#2)

C. must be understood by all employees in the unit
D. are primarily for management's needs since insurance regulations mandate them

11. It is sometimes considered desirable for a supervisor to survey the opinions of his employees before taking action on decisions affecting them.
Of the following the greatest DISADVANTAGE of following this approach is that the employees might
    A. use this opportunity to complain rather than to make constructive suggestions
    B. lose respect for their supervisor whom they feel cannot make his own decisions
    C. regard this as an attempt by the supervisor to get ideas for which he can later claim credit
    D. be resentful if their suggestions are not adopted

11.____

12. Of the following, the MOST important reason for keeping statements of duties of employees up-to-date is to
    A. serve as a basis of information for other governmental jurisdictions
    B. enable the department of personnel to develop job-related examinations
    C. differentiate between levels within the occupational groups
    D. enable each employee to know what his duties are

12.____

13. Of the following, the BEST way to evaluate the progress of a new subordinate is to
    A. compare the output of the new employee from week to week as to quantity and quality
    B. obtain the opinions of the new employee's co-workers
    C. test the new employee periodically to see how much he has learned
    D. hold frequent discussions with the employee focusing on his work

13.____

14. Of the following, a supervisor is LEAST likely to contribute to good morale in the unit if he
    A. encourages employees to increase their knowledge and proficiency in their work on their own time
    B. reprimands subordinates uniformly when infractions are committed
    C. refuses to accept explanations for mistakes regardless of who has made them or how serious they are
    D. compliments subordinates for superior work performance in the presence of their peers

14.____

15. The practice of promoting supervisors from within a given unit only, rather than from within the entire agency, may BEST be described as
    A. *desirable*, because the type of work in each unit generally is substantially different from all other units
    B. *undesirable*, since it will severely reduce the number of eligible from which to select a supervisor

15.____

C. *desirable*, since it enables each employee to know in advance the precise extent of promotion opportunities in his unit
D. *undesirable*, because it creates numerous administrative and budgetary difficulties

16. Of the following, the BEST way for a supervisor to make assignments GENERALLY is to
    A. give the easier assignments to employees with greater seniority
    B. give the difficult assignments to the employees with greater seniority
    C. make assignments according to the ability of each employee
    D. rotate the assignments among the employees

17. Assume that a supervisor makes a proposal through appropriate channels which would delegate final authority and responsibility to a subordinate employee for a major control function within the agency.
    According to current management theory, this proposal should be
    A. *adopted*, since this would enable the supervisor to devote more time to non-routine tasks
    B. *rejected*, since final responsibility for this high-level assignment may not properly be delegated to a subordinate employee
    C. *adopted*, since the assignment of increased responsibility to subordinate employees is a vital part of their development and training
    D. *rejected*, since the morale of the subordinate employees not selected for this assignment would be adversely affected

18. If it becomes necessary for a supervisor to improve the performance of a subordinate to assure the achievement of results according to plans, the BEST course of action, of the following, generally would be to
    A. emphasize the subordinate's strengths and try to motivate the employee to improve on those factors
    B. emphasize the subordinate's weak areas of performance and try to bring them up to an acceptable standard
    C. issue a memorandum to all employees warning that if performance does not improve, disciplinary measures will be taken
    D. transfer the subordinate to another section engaged in different work

19. A supervisor who specifies each phase of a job in detail supervises closely and permits very little discretion in performance of tasks GENERALLY
    A. provides motivation for his staff to produce more work
    B. finds that his subordinate make fewer mistakes than those with minimal supervision
    C. finds that his subordinates have little or no incentive to work any harder than necessary
    D. provides superior training opportunities for his employees

20. Assume that you supervise two employees who do not get along well with each other. Their relationship has been continuously deteriorating. You decide to take steps to solve this problem by first determining the reason for their inability to get along with each other.
This course of action is
   A. *desirable*, because their work is probably adversely affected by their differences
   B. *undesirable*, because your inquiries might be misinterpreted by the employees and cause resentment
   C. *desirable*, because you could then learn who is at fault for causing the deteriorating relationship and take appropriate disciplinary measures
   D. *undesirable*, because it is best to let them work their differences out between themselves

21. Routine procedures that have worked well in the past should be reviewed periodically by a supervisor MAINLY because
   A. they may have become outdated or in need of revision
   B. employees may dislike the procedures even though they have proven successful in the past
   C. these reviews are the main part of a supervisor's job
   D. this practice serves to give the supervisor an idea of how productive his subordinates are

22. Assume that an employee tells his supervisor about a grievance he has against a co-worker. The supervisor assures the employee that he will immediately take action to eliminate the grievance.
The supervisor's attitude should be considered
   A. *correct*, because a good supervisor is one who can come to a quick decision
   B. *incorrect*, because the supervisor should have told the employee that he will investigate the grievance and then determine a future course of action
   C. *correct*, because the employee's morale will be higher, resulting in greater productivity
   D. *incorrect*, because the supervisor should remain uninvolved and let the employees settle grievances between themselves

23. If an employee's work output is low and of poor quality due to faulty work habits, the MOST constructive of the following ways for a supervisor to correct this situation *generally* is to
   A. discipline the employee
   B. transfer the employee to another unit
   C. provide additional training
   D. check the employee's work continuously

24. Assume that it becomes necessary for a supervisor to ask his staff to work overtime.
Which one of the following techniques is MOST likely to win their willing cooperation to do this?

A. Point out that this is part of their job specification entitled "performs related work"
B. Explain the reason it is necessary for the employees to work overtime
C. Promise the employees special consideration regarding future leave matters
D. Warn that if the employees do not work overtime, they will face possible disciplinary action

25. If an employee's work performance has recently fallen below established minimum standards for quality and quantity, the threat of demotion or other disciplinary measures as an attempt to improve this employee's performance would probably be the MOST acceptable and effective course of action
    A. *only* after other more constructive measures have failed
    B. *if* applied uniformly to all employees as soon as performance falls below standard
    C. *only* if the employee understands that the threat will not actually be carried out
    D. *if* the employee is promised that, as soon as his work performance improves, he will be reinstated to his previous status

25.____

KEY (CORRECT ANSWERS)

1.	C		11.	D
2.	B		12.	D
3.	B		13.	A
4.	D		14.	C
5.	A		15.	B
6.	A		16.	C
7.	B		17.	B
8.	B		18.	B
9.	A		19.	C
10.	C		20.	A

21. A
22. B
23. C
24. B
25. A

TEST 3

DIRECTIONS: Each question or incomplete statement is followed by several suggested answers or completions. Select the one that BEST answers the question or completes the statement. *PRINT THE LETTER OF THE CORRECT ANSWER IN THE SPACE AT THE RIGHT.*

1. If, as a supervisor, it becomes necessary for you to assign an employee to supervise your unit during your vacation, it would generally be BEST to select the employee who
   A. is the best technician on the staff
   B. can get the work out smoothly, without friction
   C. has the most seniority
   D. is the most popular with the group

   1._____

2. Assume that, as a supervisor, your own work has accumulated to the point where you decide that it is desirable for you to delegate in order to meet your deadlines.
   The one of the following tasks which would be MOST appropriate to delegate to a subordinate is
   A. checking the work of the employees for accuracy
   B. attending a staff conference at which implementation of a new departmental policy will be discussed
   C. preparing a final report including a recommendation on purchase of expensive new laboratory equipment
   D. preparing final budget estimates for next year's budget

   2._____

3. Of the following actions, the one LEAST appropriate for you to take during an initial interview with a new employee is to
   A. find out about the experience and education of the new employee
   B. attempt to determine for what job in your unit the employee would best be suited
   C. tell the employee about his duties and responsibilities
   D. ascertain whether the employee will make good promotion material

   3._____

4. If it becomes necessary to reprimand a subordinate employee, the BEST of the following ways to do this is to
   A. ask the employee to stay after working hours and then reprimand him
   B. reprimand the employee immediately after the infraction has been committed
   C. take the employee aside and speak to him privately during regular working hours
   D. write a short memo to the employee warning that strict adherence to departmental policy and procedures is required of all employees

   4._____

5. If you, as a supervisor, believe that one of your subordinate employees has a serious problem, such as alcoholism or an emotional disturbance, which is adversely affecting his work, the BEST way to handle this situation *initially* would be to

   5._____

A. urge him to seek proper professional help before he is dismissed from his job
B. ignore it and let the employee work out the problem himself
C. suggest that the employee take an extended leave of absence until he can again function effectively
D. frankly tell the employee that unless his work improves, you will take disciplinary measures against him

6. Of the following, the BEST way to develop a subordinate's potential is to 6.____
    A. give him a fair chance to learn by doing
    B. assign him more than his share of work
    C. criticize only his work
    D. urge him to do his work rapidly

7. During a survey, an employee from another agency asks you to assist him on a job which would require a full day of your time. 7.____
    Of the following, the BEST immediate action for you to take is to
    A. refuse to assist him
    B. ask for compensation before doing it
    C. assist him promptly
    D. notify his department head

8. Of the following, the BEST way to handle an overly talkative subordinate is to 8.____
    A. have your superior talk to him about it
    B. have a subordinate talk to him about it
    C. talk to him about it in a group conference
    D. talk to him about it in private

9. While you are making a survey, a citizen questions you about the work you are doing. 9.____
    Of the following, the BEST thing to do is to
    A. answer the questions tactfully
    B. refuse to answer any questions
    C. advise him to write a letter to the main office
    D. answer the questions in double-talk

10. Respect for a supervisor is MOST likely to increase if he is 10.____
    A. morose B. sporadic C. vindictive D. zealous

11. A subordinate who continuously bypasses his immediate supervisor for technical information should be 11.____
    A. reprimanded by his immediate supervisor
    B. ignored by his immediate supervisor
    C. given more difficult work to do
    D. given less difficult work to do

12. Complicated instructions should NOT be written 12.____
    A. accurately B. lucidly C. factually D. verbosely

13. Of the following, the MOST important reason for checking a report is to
    A. check accuracy
    B. eliminate unnecessary sections
    C. catch mistakes
    D. check for delineation

14. Two subordinates under your supervision dislike each other to the extent that production is cut down.
    Your BEST action as a supervisor is to
    A. ignore the matter and hope for the best
    B. transfer the more aggressive man
    C. cut down on the workload
    D. talk to them together about the matter

15. One of the following characteristics which a supervisor should NOT display while explaining a job to a subordinate is
    A. enthusiasm   B. confidence   C. apathy   D. determination

16. Of the following, for BEST production of work, it should be assigned according to a person's
    A. attitude toward the work
    B. ability to do the work
    C. salary
    D. seniority

17. You receive an anonymous written complaint from a citizen about a subordinate who used abusive language.
    Of the following, your BEST course of action is to
    A. ignore the letter
    B. report it to your supervisor
    C. discuss the complaint with the subordinate privately
    D. keep the subordinate in the office

18. A supervisor should recognize that the way to get the BEST results from his instructions and assignments to the staff is to use
    A. a suggestive approach after he has decided exactly what is to be done and how
    B. the willing and cooperative staff members and avoid the hard-to-handle people
    C. care to select the persons most capable of carrying out the assignments
    D. an authoritative, non-nonsense tone when issuing instructions or giving assignments

19. As the supervisor of a unit, you find that you are spending too much of your time on routine tasks and not enough on coordinating the work of the staff or preparing necessary reports.
    Of the following, it would be MOST advisable for you to
    A. discard a great portion of the routine jobs done in the unit
    B. give some of the routine jobs to other members of the staff
    C. postpone the routine jobs and concentrate on coordinating the work of the staff
    D. delegate the job of coordinating the work to the most capable member of the staff

20. At times a supervisor may be called upon to train new employees. Suppose that you are giving such training in several sessions to be held on different days. During the first session, a trainee interrupts several times to ask questions at key points in your discussion.
    Of the following, the BEST way to handle this trainee is to
    A. advise him to pay closer attention so he can avoid asking too many questions
    B. tell him to listen without interrupting and he'll hear his questions answered
    C. answer his questions to show him that you know your field, but make a mental note that this trainee is a troublemaker
    D. answer each question fully and make certain he understands the answers

21. Employee errors can be reduced to a minimum by effective supervision and by training.
    Which of the following approaches used by a supervisor would usually be MOST effective in handling an employee who has made an avoidable and serious error for the first time?
    A. Tell the worker how other employees avoid making errors
    B. Analyze with the employee the situation leading to the error and then take whatever administrative or training steps are needed to avoid such errors
    C. Use this error as the basis for a staff meeting at which the employee's error is disclosed and discussed in an effort to improve the performance
    D. Urge the employee to modify his behavior in light of his mistake

22. Suppose that a particular staff member, formerly one of your most regular workers, has recently fallen into the habit of arriving a bit late to work several times a week. You feel that such a habit can grow consistently worse and spread to other staff members unless it is checked.
    Of the following, the BEST action for you to take, as the supervisor in charge of the unit, is to
    A. go immediately to your own supervisor, present the facts, and have this employee disciplined
    B. speak privately to this tardy employee, advise him of the need to improve his punctuality, and inform him that he'll be disciplined if late again
    C. talk to the co-worker with whom this late employee is most friendly, and ask the friend to help him solve his tardiness problem
    D. speak privately with this employee, and try to discover and deal with the reasons for the latenesses

23. A supervisor may make an assignment in the form of a request, a command, or a call for volunteers.
    It is LEAST desirable to make an assignment in the form of a request when
    A. an employee does not like the particular kind of assignment to be given
    B. the assignment requires working past the regular closing day
    C. an emergency has come up
    D. the assignment is not particularly pleasant for anybody

24. When you give a certain task that you normally perform yourself to one of your employees, it is MOST important that you
    A. lead the employee to believe that he has been chosen above others to perform this job
    B. describe the job as important even though it is merely a routine task
    C. explain the job that needs to be accomplished, but always let the employee decide how to do it
    D. tell the employee why you are delegating the job to him and explain exactly what he is to do

25. A supervisor when instructing new trainees in the routine of his unit should include a description of the department's overall objectives and programs in order to
    A. insure that individual work assignments will be completed satisfactorily
    B. create a favorable impression of his supervisory capabilities
    C. develop a better understanding of the purposes behind work assignments
    D. produce an immediate feeling of group cooperation

KEY (CORRECT ANSWERS)

1.	B	11.	A
2.	A	12.	D
3.	D	13.	C
4.	C	14.	D
5.	A	15.	C
6.	A	16.	B
7.	A	17.	C
8.	D	18.	C
9.	A	19.	B
10.	D	20.	D

21.	B
22.	D
23.	A
24.	D
25.	C

TEST 4

DIRECTIONS: Each question or incomplete statement is followed by several suggested answers or completions. Select the one that BEST answers the question or completes the statement. *PRINT THE LETTER OF THE CORRECT ANSWER IN THE SPACE AT THE RIGHT.*

1. An integral part of every supervisor's job is getting his ideas or instructions across to his staff.
   The extent of his success, if he has a reasonably competent staff, is PRIMARILY dependent on the
   A. interest of the employee
   B. intelligence of the employee
   C. reasoning behind the ideas or instructions
   D. presentation of the ideas or instructions

   1.____

2. Generally, what is the FIRST action the supervisor should take when an employee approaches him with a complaint?
   A. Review the employee's recent performance with him
   B. Use the complaint as a basis to discuss improvement of procedures
   C. Find out from the employee the details of the complaint
   D. Advise the employee to take his complaint to the head of the department

   2.____

3. Of the following, which is NOT usually considered one of the purposes of counseling an employee after an evaluation of his performance?
   A. Explaining the performance standards used by the supervisor
   B. Discussing necessary discipline action to be taken
   C. Emphasizing the employee's strengths and weaknesses
   D. Planning better utilization of the employee's strengths

   3.____

4. Assume that a supervisor, when reviewing a decision reached by one of his subordinates, finds the decision incorrect.
   Under these circumstances, it would be MOST desirable for the supervisor to
   A. correct the decision and inform the subordinate of this at a staff meeting
   B. correct the decision and suggest a more detailed analysis in the future
   C. help the employee find the reason for the correct decision
   D. refrain from assigning this type of a problem to the employee

   4.____

5. An IMPORTANT characteristic of a good supervisor is his ability to
   A. be a stern disciplinarian   B. put off the settling of grievances
   C. solve problems   D. find fault in individuals

   5.____

6. A new supervisor will BEST obtain the respect of the men assigned to him if he
   A. makes decisions rapidly and sticks to the, regardless of whether they are right or wrong
   B. makes decisions rapidly and then changes them just as rapidly if the decisions are wrong
   C. does not make any decisions unless he is absolutely sure that they are right
   D. makes his decisions after considering carefully all available information

   6.____

7. A newly appointed worker is operating at a level of performance below that of the other employees.
   In this situation, a supervisor should FIRST
   A. lower the acceptable standard for the new man
   B. find out why the new man cannot do as well as the others
   C. advise the new worker he will be dropped from the payroll at the end of the probationary period
   D. assign another new worker to assist the first man

8. Assume that you have to instruct a new man on a specific departmental operation. The new man seems unsure of what you have said.
   Of the following, the BEST way for you to determine whether the man has understood you is to
   A. have the man explain the operation to you in his own words
   B. repeat your explanation to him slowly
   C. repeat your explanation to him, using simpler wording
   D. emphasize the important parts of the operation to him

9. A supervisor realizes that he has taken an instantaneous dislike to a new worker assigned to him.
   The BEST course of action for the supervisor to take in this case is to
   A. be especially observant of the new worker's actions
   B. request that the new worker be reassigned
   C. make a special effort to be fair to the new worker
   D. ask to be transferred himself

10. A supervisor gives detailed instructions to his men as to how a certain type of job is to be done.
    One ADVANTAGE of this practice is that this will
    A. result in a more flexible operation
    B. standardize operations
    C. encourage new men to learn
    D. encourage initiative to learn

11. Of the following the one that would MOST likely be the result of poor planning is:
    A. Omissions are discovered after the work is completed
    B. During the course of normal inspection, a meter is found to be inaccessible
    C. An inspector completes his assignments for that day ahead of schedule
    D. A problem arises during an inspection and prevents an inspector from completing his day's assignments

12. Of the following, the BEST way for a supervisor to maintain good employee morale is for the supervisor to
    A. avoid correcting the employee when he makes mistakes
    B. continually praise the employee's work even when it is of average quality
    C. show that he is willing to assist in solving the employee's problems
    D. accept the employee's excuses for failure even though the excuses are not valid

13. A supervisor takes time to explain to his men why a departmental order has been issued.
    This practice is
    A. *good*, mainly because without this explanation the men will not be able to carry out the order
    B. *bad*, mainly because time will be wasted for no useful purpose
    C. *good*, because understanding the reasons behind an order will lead to more effective carrying out of the order
    D. *bad*, because men will then question every order that they receive

14. Of the following, the MOST important responsibility of a supervisor in charge of a section is to
    A. establish close personal relationships with each of his subordinates in the section
    B. insure that each subordinate in the section knows the full range of his duties and responsibilities
    C. maintain friendly relations with his immediate supervisor
    D. protect his subordinate from criticism from any source

15. The BEST way to get a good work output from employees is to
    A. hold over them the threat of disciplinary action or removal
    B. maintain a steady, unrelenting pressure on them
    C. show them that you can do anything they can do faster and better
    D. win their respect and liking, so they want to work for you

KEY (CORRECT ANSWERS)

1.	A	6.	D	11.	A
2.	C	7.	B	12.	C
3.	A	8.	A	13.	C
4.	C	9.	C	14.	B
5.	C	10.	B	15.	D

EXAMINATION SECTION
TEST 1

DIRECTIONS: Each question or incomplete statement is followed by several suggested answers or completions. Select the one that BEST answers the question or completes the statement. *PRINT THE LETTER OF THE CORRECT ANSWER IN THE SPACE AT THE RIGHT.*

1. Of the following, the one MOST important quality required of a good supervisor is
    A. ambition   B. leadership   C. friendliness   D. popularity

   1.____

2. It is often said that a supervisor can delegate authority but never responsibility. This means MOST NEARLY that
    A. a supervisor must do his own work if he expects it to be done properly
    B. a supervisor can assign someone else to do his work, but in the last analysis, the supervisor himself must take the blame for any actions followed
    C. authority and responsibility are two separate things that cannot be borne by the same person
    D. it is better for a supervisor never to delegate his authority

   2.____

3. One of your men who is a habitual complainer asks you to grant him a minor privilege.
   Before granting or denying such a request, you should consider
    A. the merits of the case
    B. that it is good for group morale to grant a request of this nature
    C. the man's seniority
    D. that to deny such a request will lower your standing with the men

   3.____

4. A supervisory practice on the part of a foreman which is MOST likely to lead to confusion and inefficiency is for him to
    A. give orders verbally directly to the man assigned to the job
    B. issue orders only in writing
    C. follow up his orders after issuing them
    D. relay his orders to the men through co-workers

   4.____

5. It would be POOR supervision on a foreman's part if he
    A. asked an experienced maintainer for his opinion on the method of doing a special job
    B. make it a policy to avoid criticizing a man in front of his co-workers
    C. consulted his assistant supervisor on unusual problems
    D. allowed a cooling-off period of several days before giving one of his men a deserved reprimand

   5.____

107

6. Of the following behavior characteristics of a supervisor, the one that is MOST likely to lower the morale of the men he supervises is
   A. diligence
   B. favoritism
   C. punctuality
   D. thoroughness

7. Of the following, the BEST method of getting an employee who is not working up to his capacity to produce more work is to
   A. have another employee criticize his production
   B. privately criticize his production but encourage him to produce more
   C. criticize his production before his associates
   D. criticize his production and threaten to fire him

8. Of the following, the BEST thing for a supervisor to do when a subordinate has done a very good job is to
   A. tell him to take it easy
   B. praise his work
   C. reduce his workload
   D. say nothing because he may become conceited

9. Your orders to your crew are MOST likely to be followed if you
   A. explain the reasons for these orders
   B. warn that all violators will be punished
   C. promise easy assignments to those who follow these orders best
   D. say that they are for the good of the department

10. In order to be a good supervisor, you should
    A. impress upon your men that you demand perfection in their work at all times
    B. avoid being blamed for your crew's mistakes
    C. impress your superior with your ability
    D. see to it that your men get what they are entitled to

11. In giving instructions to a crew, you should
    A. speak in as loud a tone as possible
    B. speak in a coaxing, persuasive manner
    C. speak quietly, clearly, and courteously
    D. always use the word *please* when giving instructions

12. Of the following factors, the one which is LEAST important in evaluating an employee and his work is his
    A. dependability
    B. quantity of work done
    C. quality of work done
    D. education and training

13. When a District Superintendent first assumes his command, it is LEAST important for him at the beginning to observe
    A. how his equipment is designed and its adaptability
    B. how to reorganize the district for greater efficiency
    C. the capabilities of the men in the district
    D. the methods of operation being employed

14. When making an inspection of one of the buildings under your supervision, the BEST procedure to follow in making a record of the inspection is to
    A. return immediately to the office and write a report from memory
    B. write down all the important facts during or as soon as you complete the inspection
    C. fix in your mind all important facts so that you can repeat them from memory if necessary
    D. fix in your mind all important facts so that you can make out your report at the end of the day

14._____

15. Assume that your superior has directed you to make certain changes in your established procedure. After using this modified procedure on several occasions, you find that the original procedure was distinctly superior and you wish to return to it.
    You should
    A. let your superior find this out for himself
    B. simply change back to the original procedure
    C. compile definite data and information to prove your case to your superior
    D. persuade one of the more experienced workers to take this matter up with your superior

15._____

16. An inspector visited a large building under construction. He inspected the soil lines at 9 A.M., water lines at 10 A.M., fixtures at 11 A.M., and did his office work in the afternoon. He followed the same pattern daily for weeks.
    This procedure was
    A. *good*, because it was methodical and he did not miss anything
    B. *good*, because it gave equal time to all phases of the plumbing
    C. *bad*, because not enough time was devoted to fixtures
    D. *bad*, because the tradesmen knew when the inspection would occur

16._____

17. Assume that one of the foremen in a training course, which you are conducting, proposes a poor solution for a maintenance problem.
    Of the following, the BEST course of action for you to take is to
    A. accept the solution tentatively and correct it during the next class meeting
    B. point out all the defects of this proposed solution and wait until somebody thinks of a better solution
    C. try to get the class to reject this proposed solution and develop a better solution
    D. let the matter pass since somebody will present a better solution as the class work proceeds

17._____

18. As a supervisor, you should be seeking ways to improve the efficiency of shop operations by means such as changing established work procedures.
    The following are offered as possible actions that you should consider in changing established work procedures:
    I. Make changes only when your foremen agree to them
    II. Discuss changes with your supervisor before putting them into practice

18._____

III. Standardize any operation which is performed on a continuing basis
IV. Make changes quickly and quietly in order to avoid dissent
V. Secure expert guidance before instituting unfamiliar procedures
Of the following suggested answers, the one that describes the actions to be taken to change established work procedures is
   A. I, IV, V   B. II, III, V   C. III, IV, V   D. All of the above

19. A supervisor determined that a foreman, without informing his superior, delegated responsibility for checking time cards to a member of his gang. The supervisor then called the foreman into his office where he reprimanded the foreman.
This action of the supervisor in reprimanding the foreman was
   A. *proper*, because the checking of time cards is the foreman's responsibility and should not be delegated
   B. *proper*, because the foreman did not ask the supervisor for permission to delegate responsibility
   C. *improper*, because the foreman may no longer take the initiative in solving future problems
   D. *improper*, because the supervisor is interfering in a function which is not his responsibility

20. A capable supervisor should check all operations under his control.
Of the following, the LEAST important reason for doing this is to make sure that
   A. operations are being performed as scheduled
   B. he personally observes all operations at all times
   C. all the operations are still needed
   D. his manpower is being utilized efficiently

21. A supervisor makes it a practice to apply fair and firm discipline in all cases of rule infractions, including those of a minor nature.
This practice should PRIMARILY be considered
   A. *bad*, since applying discipline for minor violations is a waste of time
   B. *good*, because not applying discipline for minor infractions can lead to a more serious erosion of discipline
   C. *bad*, because employees do not like to be disciplined for minor violations of the rules
   D. *good*, because violating any rule can cause a dangerous situation to occur

22. A maintainer would PROPERLY consider it poor supervisory practice for a foreman to consult with him on
   A. which of several repair jobs should be scheduled first
   B. how to cope with personal problems at home
   C. whether the neatness of his headquarters can be improved
   D. how to express a suggestion which the maintainer plans to submit formally

23. Assume that you have determined that the work of one of your foremen and the men he supervises is consistently behind schedule. When you discuss this situation with the foreman, he tells you that his men are poor workers and then complains that he must spend all of his time checking on their work.
The following actions are offered for your consideration as possible ways of solving the problem of poor performance of the foreman and his men:
I. Review the work standards with the foreman and determine whether they are realistic.
II. Tell the foreman that you will recommend him for the foreman's training course for retraining.
III. Ask the foreman for the names of the maintainers and then replace them as soon as possible.
IV. Tell the foreman that you expect him to meet a satisfactory level of performance.
V. Tell the foreman to insist that his men work overtime to catch up to the schedule.
VI. Tell the foreman to review the type and amount of training he has given the maintainers.
VII. Tell the foreman that he will be out of a job if he does not produce on schedule.
VIII. Avoid all criticism of the foreman and his methods.
Which of the following suggested answers CORRECTLY lists the proper actions to be taken to solve the problem of poor performance of the foreman and his men?
A. I, II, IV, VI   B. I, III, V, VII   C. II, III, VI, VIII   D. IV, V, VI, VIII

23.____

24. When a conference or a group discussion is tending to turn into a *bull session* without constructive purpose, the BEST action to take is to
A. reprimand the leader of the bull session
B. redirect the discussion to the business at hand
C. dismiss the meeting and reschedule it for another day
D. allow the bull session to continue

24.____

25. Assume that you have been assigned responsibility for a program in which a high production rate is mandatory. From past experience, you know that your foremen do not perform equally well in the various types of jobs given to them. Which of the following methods should you use in selecting foremen for the specific types of work involved in the program?
A. Leave the method of selecting foremen to your supervisor
B. Assign each foreman to the work he does best
C. Allow each foreman to choose his own job
D. Assign each foreman to a job which will permit him to improve his own abilities

25.____

KEY (CORRECT ANSWERS)

1.	B		11.	C
2.	B		12.	D
3.	A		13.	B
4.	D		14.	B
5.	D		15.	C
6.	B		16.	D
7.	B		17.	C
8.	B		18.	B
9.	A		19.	A
10.	D		20.	B

21. B
22. A
23. A
24. B
25. B

TEST 2

DIRECTIONS: Each question or incomplete statement is followed by several suggested answers or completions. Select the one that BEST answers the question or completes the statement. *PRINT THE LETTER OF THE CORRECT ANSWER IN THE SPACE AT THE RIGHT.*

1. A foreman who is familiar with modern management principles should know that the one of the following requirements of an administrator which is LEAST important is his ability to
    A. coordinate work
    B. plan, organize, and direct the work under his control
    C. cooperate with others
    D. perform the duties of the employees under his jurisdiction

    1.____

2. When subordinates request his advice in solving problems encountered in their work, a certain chief occasionally answers the request by first asking the subordinate what he thinks should be done.
    This action by the chief is, on the whole,
    A. *desirable*, because it stimulates subordinates to give more thought to the solution of problems encountered
    B. *undesirable*, because it discourages subordinates from asking questions
    C. *desirable*, because it discourages subordinates from asking questions
    D. *undesirable*, because it undermines the confidence of subordinates in the ability of their supervisor

    2.____

3. Of the following factors that may be considered by a unit head in dealing with the tardy subordinate, the one which should be given LEAST consideration is the
    A. frequency with which the employee is tardy
    B. effect of the employee's tardiness upon the work of other employees
    C. willingness of the employee to work overtime when necessary
    D. cause of the employee's tardiness

    3.____

4. The MOST important requirement of a good inspectional report is that it should be
    A. properly addressed   B. lengthy
    C. clear and brief   D. spelled correctly

    4.____

5. Building superintendents frequently inquire about departmental inspectional procedures.
    Of the following, it is BEST to
    A. advise them to write to the department for an official reply
    B. refuse as the inspectional procedure is a restricted matter
    C. briefly explain the procedure to them
    D. avoid the inquiry by changing the subject

    5.____

6. Reprimanding a crew member before other workers is a
   A. *good* practice; the reprimand serves as a warning to the other workers
   B. *bad* practice; people usually resent criticism made in public
   C. *good* practice; the other workers will realize that the supervisor is fair
   D. *bad* practice; the other workers will take sides in the dispute

7. Of the following actions, the one which is LEAST likely to promote good work is for the group leader to
   A. praise workers for doing a good job
   B. call attention to the opportunities for promotion for better workers
   C. threaten to recommend discharge of workers who are below standard
   D. put into practice any good suggestion made by crew members

8. A supervisor notices that a member of his crew has skipped a routine step in his job.
   Of the following, the BEST action for the supervisor to take is to
   A. promptly question the worker about the incident
   B. immediately assign another man to complete the job
   C. bring up the incident the next time the worker asks for a favor
   D. say nothing about the incident but watch the worker carefully in the future

9. Assume you have been told to show a new worker how to operate a piece of equipment.
   Your FIRST step should be to
   A. ask the worker if he has any questions about the equipment
   B. permit the worker to operate the equipment himself while you carefully watch to prevent damage
   C. demonstrate the operation of the equipment for the worker
   D. have the worker read an instruction booklet on the maintenance of the equipment

10. Whenever a new man was assigned to his crew, the supervisor would introduce him to all other crew members, take him on a tour of the plant, tell him about bus schedules and places to eat.
    This practice is
    A. *good*; the new man is made to feel welcome
    B. *bad*; supervisors should not interfere in personal matters
    C. *good*; the new man knows that he can bring his personal problems to the supervisor
    D. *bad*; work time should not be spent on personal matters

11. The MOST important factor in successful leadership is the ability to
    A. obtain instant obedience to all orders
    B. establish friendly personal relations with crew members
    C. avoid disciplining crew members
    D. make crew members want to do what should be done

12. Explaining the reasons for departmental procedure to workers tends to
    A. waste time which should be used for productive purposes
    B. increase their interest in their work
    C. make them more critical of departmental procedures
    D. confuse them

13. If you want a job done well do it yourself.
    For a supervisor to follow this advice would be
    A. *good*; a supervisor is responsible for the work of his crew
    B. *bad*; a supervisor should train his men, not do their work
    C. *good*; a supervisor should be skilled in all jobs assigned to his crew
    D. *bad*; a supervisor loses respect when he works with his hands

14. When a supervisor discovers a mistake in one of the jobs for which his crew is responsible, it is MOST important for him to find out
    A. whether anybody else knows about the mistake
    B. who was to blame for the mistake
    C. how to prevent similar mistakes in the future
    D. whether similar mistakes occurred in the past

15. A supervisor who has to explain a new procedure to his crew should realize that questions from the crew USUALLY show that they
    A. are opposed to the new practice
    B. are completely confused by the explanation
    C. need more training in the new procedure
    D. are interested in the explanation

16. A good way for a supervisor to retain the confidence of his or her employees is to
    A. say as little as possible
    B. check work frequently
    C. make no promises unless they will be fulfilled
    D. never hesitate in giving an answer to any question

17. Good supervision is ESSENTIALLY a matter of
    A. patience in supervising workers   B. care in selecting workers
    C. skill in human relations   D. fairness in disciplining workers

18. It is MOST important for an employee who has been assigned a monotonous task to
    A. perform this task before doing other work
    B. ask another employee to help
    C. perform this task only after all other work has been completed
    D. take measures to prevent mistakes in performing the task

19. One of your employees has violated a minor agency regulation.
    The FIRST thing you should do is
    A. warn the employee that you will have to take disciplinary action if it should happen again
    B. ask the employee to explain his or her actions
    C. inform your supervisor and wait for advice
    D. write a memo describing the incident and place it in the employee's personnel file

20. One of your employees tells you that he feels you give him much more work than the other employees, and he is having trouble meeting your deadlines.
    You should
    A. ask if he has been under a lot of non-work related stress lately
    B. review his recent assignments to determine if he is correct
    C. explain that this is a busy time, but you are dividing the work equally
    D. tell him that he is the most competent employee and that is why he receives more work

21. A supervisor assigns one of his crew to complete a portion of a job. A short time later, the supervisor notices that the portion has not been completed.
    Of the following, the BEST way for the supervisor to handle this is to
    A. ask the crew member why he has not completed the assignment
    B. reprimand the crew member for not obeying orders
    C. assign another crew member to complete the assignment
    D. complete the assignment himself

22. Supposes that a member of your crew complains that you are *playing favorites* in assigning work.
    Of the following, the BEST method of handling the complaint is to
    A. deny it and refuse to discuss the matter with the worker
    B. take the opportunity to tell the worker what is wrong with his work
    C. ask the worker for examples to prove his point and try to clear up any misunderstanding
    D. promise to be more careful in making assignments in the future

23. A member of your crew comes to you with a complaint. After discussing the matter with him, it is clear that you have convinced him that his complaint was not justified.
    At this point, you should
    A. permit him to drop the matter
    B. make him admit his error
    C. pretend to see some justification in his complaint
    D. warn him against making unjustified complaints

24. Suppose that a supervisor has in his crew an older man who works rather slowly. In other respects, this man is a good worker; he is seldom absent, works carefully, never loafs, and is cooperative.

The BEST way for the supervisor to handle this worker is to
- A. try to get him to work faster and less carefully
- B. give him the most disagreeable job
- C. request that he be given special training
- D. permit him to work at his own speed

25. Suppose that a member of your crew comes to you with a suggestion he thinks will save time in doing a job. You realize immediately that it won't work. Under these circumstances, your BEST action would be to
    - A. thank the worker for the suggestion and forget about it
    - B. explain to the worker why you think it won't work
    - C. tell the worker to put the suggestion in writing
    - D. ask the other members of your crew to criticize the suggestion

25.____

KEY (CORRECT ANSWERS)

1.	D		11.	D
2.	A		12.	B
3.	C		13.	B
4.	C		14.	C
5.	C		15.	D
6.	B		16.	C
7.	C		17.	C
8.	A		18.	D
9.	C		19.	B
10.	A		20.	B

21.	A
22.	C
23.	A
24.	D
25.	B

SUPERVISION STUDY GUIDE

Social science has developed information about groups and leadership in general and supervisor-employee relationships in particular. Since organizational effectiveness is closely linked to the ability of supervisors to direct the activities of employees, these findings are important to executives everywhere.

IS A SUPERVISOR A LEADER?

First-line supervisors are found in all large business and government organizations. They are the men at the base of an organizational hierarchy. Decisions made by the head of the organization reach them through a network of intermediate positions. They are frequently referred to as part of the management team, but their duties seldom seem to support this description.

A supervisor of clerks, tax collectors, meat inspectors, or securities analysts is not charged with budget preparation. He cannot hire or fire the employees in his own unit on his say-so. He does not administer programs which require great planning, coordinating, or decision making.

Then what is he? He is the man who is directly in charge of a group of employees doing productive work for a business or government agency. If the work requires the use of machines, the men he supervises operate them. If the work requires the writing of reports, the men he supervises write them. He is expected to maintain a productive flow of work without creating problems which higher levels of management must solve. But is he a leader?

To carry out a specific part of an agency's mission, management creates a unit, staffs it with a group of employees and designates a supervisor to take charge of them. Management directs what this unit shall do, from time to time changes directions, and often indicates what the group should not do. Management presumably creates status for the supervisor by giving him more pay, a title, and special privileges.

Management asks a supervisor to get his workers to attain organizational goals, including the desired quantity and quality of production. Supposedly, he has authority to enable him to achieve this objective. Management at least assumes that by establishing the status of the supervisor's position, it has created sufficient authority to enable him to achieve these goals—not his goals, nor necessarily the group's, but management's goals.

In addition, supervision includes writing reports, keeping records of membership in a higher-level administrative group, industrial engineering, safety engineering, editorial duties, housekeeping duties, etc. The supervisor as a member of an organizational network, must be responsible to the changing demands of the management above him. At the same time, he must be responsive to the demands of the work group of which he is a member. He is placed in the difficult position of communicating and implementing new decisions, changed programs and revised production quotas for his work group, although he may have had little part in developing them.

It follows, then, that supervision has a special characteristic: achievement of goals, previously set by management, through the efforts of others. It is in this feature of the supervisor's job that we find the role of a leader in the sense of the following definition: *A leader is that person who <u>most</u> effectively influences group activities toward goal setting and goal achievements.*

This definition is broad. It covers both leaders in groups that come together voluntarily and in those brought together through a work assignment in a factory, store, or government agency. In the natural group, the authority necessary to attain goals is determined by the group membership and is granted by them. In the working group, it is apparent that the establishment of a supervisory position creates a predisposition on the part of employees to accept the authority of the occupant of that position. We cannot, however, assume that mere occupation confers authority sufficient to assure the accomplishment of an organization's goals.

Supervision is different, then, from leadership. The supervisor is expected to fulfill the role of leader but without obtaining a grant of authority from the group he supervises. The supervisor is expected to influence the group in the achieving of goals but is often handicapped by having little influence on the organizational process by which goals are set. The supervisor, because he works in an organizational setting, has the burdens of additional organizational duties and restrictions and requirements arising out of the fact that his position is subordinate to a hierarchy of higher-level supervisors. These differences between leadership and supervision are reflected in our definition: *Supervision is basically a leadership role, in a formal organization, which has as its objective the effective influencing of other employees.*

Even though these differences between supervision and leadership exist, a significant finding of experimenters in this field is that supervisors <u>must</u> be leaders to be successful.

The problem is: How can a supervisor exercise leadership in an organizational setting? We might say that the supervisor is expected to be a natural leader in a situation which does not come about naturally. His situation becomes really difficult in an organization which is more eager to make its supervisors into followers rather than leaders.

LEADERSHIP: NATURAL AND ORGANIZATIONAL

Leadership, in its usual sense of *natural* leadership, and supervision are not the same. In some cases, leadership embraces broader powers and functions than supervision; in other cases, supervision embraces more than leadership. This is true both because of the organization and technical aspects of the supervisor's job and because of the relatively freer setting and inherent authority of the natural leader.

The natural leader usually has much more authority and influence than the supervisor. Group members not only follow his command but prefer it that way. The employee, however, can appeal the supervisor's commands to his union or to the supervisor's superior or to the personnel office. These intercessors represent restrictions on the supervisor's power to lead.

The natural leader can gain greater membership involvement in the group's objectives, and he can change the objectives of the group. The supervisor can attempt to gain employee support only for management's objectives; he cannot set other objectives. In these instances leadership is broader than supervision.

The natural leader must depend upon whatever skills are available when seeking to attain objectives. The supervisor is trained in the administrative skills necessary to achieve management's goals. If he does not possess the requisite skills, however, he can call upon management's technicians.

A natural leader can maintain his leadership, in certain groups, merely by satisfying members' need for group affiliation. The supervisor must maintain his leadership by directing and organizing his group to achieve specific organizational goals set for him and his group by management. He must have a technical competence and a kind of coordinating ability which is not needed by many natural leaders.

A natural leader is responsible only to his group which grants him authority. The supervisor is responsible to management, which employs him, and also to the work group of which he is a member. The supervisor has the exceedingly difficult job of reconciling the demands of two groups frequently in conflict. He is often placed in the untenable position of trying to play two antagonistic roles. In the above instance, supervision is broader than leadership.

ORGANIZATIONAL INFLUENCES ON LEADERSHIP

The supervisor is both a product and a prisoner of the organization wherein we find him. The organization which creates the supervisor's position also obstructs, restricts, and channelizes the exercise of his duties. These influences extend beyond prescribed functional relationships to specific supervisory behavior. For example, even in a face-to-face situation involving one of his subordinates, the supervisor's actions are controlled to a great extent by his organization. His behavior must conform to the organization policy on human relations, rules which dictate personnel procedures, specific prohibitions governing conduct, the attitudes of his own superior, etc. He is not a free agent operating within the limits of his work group. His freedom of action is much more circumscribed than is generally admitted. The organizational influences which limit his leadership actions can be classified as structure, prescriptions, and proscriptions.

The organizational structure places each supervisor's position in context with other designated positions. It determines the relationships between his position and specific positions which impinge on his. The structure of the organization designates a certain position to which he looks for orders and information about his work. It gives a particular status to his position within a pattern of statuses from which he perceives that (1) certain positions are on a par, organizationally, with his, (2) other positions are subordinate, and (3) still others are superior.

The organizational structure determines those positions to which he should look for advice and assistance, and those positions to which he should give advice and assistance.

For instance, the organizational structure has predetermined that the supervisor of a clerical processing unit shall report to a supervisory position in a higher echelon. He shall have certain relationships with the supervisors of the work units which transmit work to and receive work from his unit. He shall discuss changes and clarification of procedures with certain staff units, such as organization and methods, cost accounting, and personnel. He shall consult supervisors of units which provide or receive special work assignments.

The organizational structure, however, establishes patterns other than those of the relationships of positions. These are the patterns of responsibility, authority, and expectations.

The supervisor is responsible for certain activities or results; he is presumably invested with the authority to achieve these. His set of authority and responsibility is interwoven with other sets to the end that all goals and functions of the organization are parceled out in small, manageable lots. This, of course, establishes a series of expectations: a single supervisor can perform his particular set of duties only upon the assumption that preceding or contiguous sets of duties have been, or are being carried out. At the same time, he is aware of the expectations of others that he will fulfill his functional role.

The structure of an organization establishes relationships between specified positions and specific expectations for these positions. The fact that these relationships and expectations are established is one thing; whether or not they are met is another.

PRESCRIPTIONS AND PROSCRIPTIONS

But let us return to the organizational influences which act to restrict the supervisor's exercise of leadership. These are the prescriptions and proscriptions generally in effect in all organizations, and those peculiar to a single organization. In brief these are the *thou shalt's* and the *thou shalt not's*.

Organizations not only prescribe certain duties for individual supervisory positions, they also prescribe specific methods and means of carrying out these duties and maintaining management-employee relations. These include rules, regulations, policy, and tradition. It does no good for the supervisor to say, *This seems to be the best way to handle such-and-such,* if the organization has established a routine for dealing with problems. For good or bad, there are rules that state that firings shall be executed in such a manner, accompanied by a certain notification; that training shall be conducted, and in this manner. Proscriptions are merely negative prescriptions; you may not discriminate against any employee because of politics or race; you shall not suspend any employee without following certain procedures and obtaining certain approvals.

Most of these prohibitions and rules apply to the area of interpersonal relations, precisely the area which is now arousing most interest on the part of administrators and managers. We have become concerned about the contrast between formally prescribed relationships and interpersonal relationships, and this brings us to the often discussed informal organization.

FORMAL AND INFORMAL ORGANIZATIONS

As we well know, the functions and activities of any organization are broken down into individual units of work called positions. Administrators must establish a pattern which will link these positions to each other and relate them to a system of authority and responsibility. Man-to-man are spelled out as plainly as possible for all to understand. Managers, then, build an official structure which we call the formal organization.

In these same organizations, employees react individually and in groups to institutionally determined roles. John, a worker, rides in the same carpool as Joe, a foreman. An unplanned communication develops. Harry, a machinist knows more about high-speed machining than his foreman or anyone else in his shop. An unofficial tool boss comes into being. Mary, who fought with Jane, is promoted over her. Jane now gives Mary's directions. A planned relationship fails to develop. The employees have built a structure which we call the informal organization.

Formal organization is a system of management-prescribed relations between positions in an organization.

Informal organization is a network of unofficial relations between people in an organization.

These definitions might lead us to the absurd conclusion that positions carry out formal activities and that employe4es spend their time in unofficial activities. We must recognize that organizational activities are in all cases carried out by people. The formal structure provides a needed framework within which interpersonal relations occur. What we call informal organization is the complex of normal, natural relations among employees. These personal relationships may be negative or positive. That is, they may impede or aid the achievement of organizational goals. For example, friendship between two supervisors greatly increases the probability of good cooperation and coordination between their sections. On the other hand, *buck passing* nullifies the formal structure by failure to meet a prescribed and expected responsibility.

It is improbable that an ideal organization exists where all activities are carried out in strict conformity to a formally prescribed pattern of functional roles. Informal organization arises because of the incompleteness and ambiguities in the network of formally prescribed relationships, or in response to the needs or inadequacies of supervisors or managers who hold prescribed functional roles in an organization. Many of these relationships are not prescribed by the organizational pattern; many cannot be prescribed; many should not be prescribed.

Management faces the problem of keeping the informal organization in harmony with the mission of the agency. One way to do this is to make sure that all employees have a clear understanding of and are sympathetic with that mission. The issuance of organizational charts, procedural manuals, and functional descriptions of the work to be done by divisions and sections helps communicate management's plans and goals. Issuances alone, of course, cannot do the whole job. They should be accompanied by oral discussion and explanation. Management must ensure that there is mutual understanding and acceptance of charts and procedures. More important is that management acquaint itself with the attitudes, activities, and peculiar brands of logic which govern the informal organization. Only through this type of knowledge can they and supervisors keep informal goals consistent with the agency mission.

SUPERVISION STATUS AND FUNCTIONAL ROLE

A well-established supervisor is respected by the employees who work with him. They defer to his wishes. It is clear that a superior-subordinate relationship has been established. That is, status of the supervisor has been established in relation to other employees of the same work group. This same supervisor gains the respect of employees when he behaves in as certain manner. He will be expected, generally, to follow the customs of the group in such matters as dress, recreation, and manner of speaking. The group has a set of expectations as to his behavior. His position is a functional role which carries with it a collection of rights and obligations.

The position of supervisor usually has a status distinct from the individual who occupies it: it is much like a position description which exists whether or not there is an incumbent. The status of a supervisory position is valued higher than that of an employee position both because of the functional role of leadership which is assigned to it and because of the status symbols of titles, rights, and privileges which go with it.

Social ranking, or status, is not simple because it involves both the position and the man. An individual may be ranked higher than others because of his education, social background, perceived leadership ability, or conformity to group customs and ideals. If such a man is ranked higher by the members of a work group than their supervisor, the supervisor's effectiveness may be seriously undermined.

If the organization does not build and reinforce a supervisor's status, his position can be undermined in a different way. This will happen when managers go around rather than through the supervisor or designate him as a straw boss, acting boss, or otherwise not a real boss.

Let us clarify this last point. A role, and corresponding status, establishes a set of expectations. Employees expect their supervisor to do certain things and to act in certain ways. They are prepared to respond to that expected behavior. When the supervisor's behavior does not conform to their expectations, they are surprised, confused, and ill-at-ease. It becomes necessary for them to resolve their confusion, if they can. They might do this by turning to one of their own members for leadership. If the confusion continues, or their attempted solutions are not satisfactory, they will probably become a poorly motivated, non-cohesive group which cannot function very well.

COMMUNICATION AND THE SUPERVISOR

In a recent survey, railroad workers reported that they rarely look to their supervisor for information about the company. This is startling, at least to us, because we ordinarily think of the supervisor as the link between management and worker. We expect the supervisor to be the prime source of information about the company. Actually, the railroad workers listed the supervisor next to last in the o5rder of their sources of information. Most surprising of all, the supervisors, themselves, stated that rumor and unofficial contacts were their principal sources of information. Here we see one of the reasons why supervisors may not be as effective as management desires.

The supervisor is not only being bypassed by his work group, he is being ignored, and his position weakened, by the very organization which is holding him responsible for the activities of his workers. If he is management's representative to the employee, then management has an obligation to keep him informed of its activities. This is necessary if he is to carry out his functions efficiently and maintain his leadership in the work group. The supervisor is expected to be a source of information; when he is not, his status is not clear, and employees are dissatisfied because he has not lived up to expectations.

By providing information to the supervisor to pass along to employees, we can strengthen his position as leader of the group, and increase satisfaction and cohesion within the group. Because he has more information than the other members, receives information sooner, and passes it along at the proper times, members turn to him as a source and also provide him with information in the hope of receiving some in return. From this, we can see an increase in group cohesiveness because:

- Employees are bound closer to their supervisor because he is *in the know*.
- There is less need to go outside the group for answers
- Employees will more quickly turn to the supervisor for enlightenment

The fact that he has the answers will also enhance the supervisor's standing in the eyes of his men. This increased status will serve to bolster his authority and control of the group and will probably result in improved morale and productivity.

The foregoing, of course, does not mean that all management information should be given out. There are obviously certain policy determinations and discussions which need not or cannot be transmitted to all supervisors. However, the supervisor must be kept as fully informed as possible so that he can answer questions when asked and can allay needless fears and anxieties. Further, the supervisor has the responsibility of encouraging employee questions and submissions of information. He must be able to present information to employees so that it is clearly understood and accepted. His attitude and manner should make it clear that he believes in what he is saying, that the information is necessary or desirable to the group, and that he is prepared to act on the basis of the information.

SUPERVISION AND JOB PERFORMANCE

The productivity of work groups is a product; employees' efforts are multiplied by the supervision they receive. Many investigators have analyzed this relationship and have discovered elements of supervision which differentiate high and low production groups. These researchers have identified certain types of supervisory practices which they classify as *employee-centered* and other types which they classify as *production centered*.

The difference between these two kinds of supervision lies not in specific practices but in the approach or orientation to supervision. The employee-centered supervisor directs most of his efforts toward increasing employee motivation. He is concerned more with realizing the potential energy of persons than with administrative and technological methods of increasing efficiency and productivity. He is the man who finds ways of causing employees to want to work harder with the same tools. These supervisors emphasize the personal relations between their employees and themselves.

Now, obviously, these pictures are overdrawn. No one supervisor has all the virtues of the ideal type of employee-centered supervisor. And, fortunately, no one supervisor has all the bad traits found in many production-centered supervisors. We should remember that the various practices that researchers have fond which distinguish these two kinds of supervision represent the many practices and methods of supervisors of all gradations between these extremes. We should be careful, too, of the implications of the labels attached to the two types. For instance, being production-centered is not necessarily bad, since the principal responsibility of any supervisor is maintaining the production level that is expected of his work group. Being employee-centered may not necessarily be good, if the only result is a happy, chuckling crew of loafers. To return to the researchers' findings, employee-centered supervisors:

- Recommend promotions, transfers, pay increases
- Inform men about what is happening in the company
- Keep men posted on how well they are doing
- Hear complaints and grievances sympathetically
- Speak up for subordinates

Production-centered supervisors, on the other hand, don't do those things. They check on employees more frequently, give more detailed and frequent instructions, don't give reasons for changes, and are more punitive when mistakes are made. Employee-centered supervisors were reported to contribute to high morale and high production, whereas production-centered supervision was associated with lower morale and less production.

More recent findings, however, show that the relationship between supervision and productivity is not this simple. Investigators now report that high production is more frequently associated with supervisory practices which combine employee-centered behavior with concern for production. (This concern is not the same, however, as anxiety about production, which is the hallmark of our production-centered supervisor.) Let us examine these apparently contradictory findings and the premises from which they are derived.

SUPERVISION AND MORALE

Why do supervisory activities cause high or low production? As the name implies, the activities of the employee-centered supervisor tend to relate him more closely and satisfactorily to his workers. The production-centered supervisor's practices tend to separate him from his group and to foster antagonism. An analysis of this difference may answer our question.

Earlier, we pointed out that the supervisor is a type of leader and that leadership is intimately related to the group in which it occurs We discover, now, that an employee-centered supervisor's primary activities are concerned with both his leadership and his group membership. Such a supervisor is a member of a group and occupies a leadership role in that group.

These facts are sometimes obscured when we speak of the supervisor as management's representative, or as the organizational link between management and the employee, or as the end of the chain of command. If we really want to understand what it is we expect of the supervisor, we must remember that he is the designated leader of a group of employees to whom he is bound by interaction and interdependence.

Most of his actions are aimed, consciously or unconsciously, at strengthening membership ties in the group. This includes both making members more conscious that he is a member of their group) and causing members to identify themselves more closely with the group. These ends are accomplished by:

- making the group more attractive to the worker: they find satisfaction of their needs for recognition, friendship, enjoyable work, etc.;
- maintaining open communication: employees can express their views and obtain information about the organization
- giving assistance: members can seek advice on personal problems as well as their work; and
- acting as a buffer between the group and management: he speaks up for his men and explains the reasons for management's decisions.

Such actions both strengthen group cohesiveness and solidarity and affirm the supervisor's leadership position in the group.

DEFINING MORALE

This brings us back to a point mentioned earlier. We had said that employee-centered supervisors contribute to high morale as well as to high production. But how can we explain units which have low morale and high productivity, or vice versa? Usually production and morale are considered separately, partly because they are measured against different criteria and partly because, in some instances, they seem to be independent of each other.

Some of this difficulty may stem from confusion over definitions of morale. Morale has been defined as, or measured by, absences from work, satisfaction with job or company, dissension among members of work groups, productivity, apathy or lack of interest, readiness to help others, and a general aura of happiness as rated by observers. Some of these criteria of morale are not subject to the influence of the supervisor, and some of them are not clearly related to productivity. Definitions like these invite findings of low morale coupled with high production.

Both productivity and morale can be influenced by environmental factors not under the control of group members or supervisors. Such things as plant layout, organizational structure and goals, lighting, ventilation, communications, and management planning may have an adverse or desirable effect.

We might resolve the dilemma by defining morale on the basis of our understanding of the supervisor as leader of a group; morale is the degree of satisfaction of group members with their leadership. In this light, the supervisor's employee-centered activities bear a clear relation to morale. His efforts to increase employee identification with the group and to strengthen his leadership lead to greater satisfaction with that leadership. By increasing group cohesiveness and by demonstrating that his influence and power can aid the group, he is able to enhance his leadership status and afford satisfaction to the group.

SUPERVISION, PRODUCTION, AND MORALE

There are factors within the organization itself which determine whether increased production is possible:

- Are production goals expressed in terms understandable to employees and are they realistic?
- Do supervisors responsible for production respect the agency mission and production goals?
- If employees do not know how to do the job well, does management provide a trainer—often the supervisor—who can teach efficient work methods?

There are other factors within the work group which determine whether increased production will be attained:

- Is leadership present which can bring about the desired level of production?
- Are production goals accepted by employees as reasonable and attainable?
- If group effort is involved, are members able to coordinate their efforts?

Research findings confirm the view that an employee-centered supervisor can achieve higher morale than a production-centered supervisor. Managers may well ask what is the relationship between this and production.

Supervision is production-oriented to the extent that it focuses attention on achieving organizational goals, and plans and devises methods for attaining them; it is employee-centered to the extent that it focuses attention on employee attitudes toward those goals, and plans and works toward maintenance of employee satisfaction.

High productivity and low morale result when a supervisor plans and organizes work efficiently but cannot achieve high membership satisfaction. Low production and high morale result when a supervisor, though keeping members satisfied with his leadership, either has not gained acceptance of organizational goals or does not have the technical competence to achieve them.

The relationship between supervision, morale, and productivity is an interdependent one, with the supervisor playing an integral role due to his ability to influence productivity and morale independently of each other.

A supervisor who can plan his work well has good technical knowledge, and who can install better production methods can raise production without necessarily increasing group satisfaction. On the other hand, a supervisor who can motivate his employees and keep them satisfied with his leadership can gain high production in spite of technical difficulties and environmental obstacles.

CLIMATE AND SUPERVISION

Climate, the intangible environment of an organization made up of attitudes, beliefs, and traditions, plays a large part in morale, productivity, and supervision. Usually when we speak of climate and its relationship to morale and productivity, we talk about the merits of *democratic* versus *authoritarian* climate. Employees seem to produce more and have higher morale in a democratic climate, whereas in an authoritarian climate, the reverse seems to be true or so the researchers tell us. We would do well to determine what these terms mean to supervision.

Perhaps most of our difficulty in understanding and applying these concepts comes from our emotional reactions to the words themselves. For example, authoritarian climate is usually painted as the very blackest kind of dictatorship. This is not surprising, because we are usually expected to believe that it is invariably bad. Conversely, democratic climate is drawn to make the driven snow look impure by comparison.

Now these descriptions are most probably true when we talk about our political processes, or town meetings, or freedom of speech. However, the same labels have been used by social scientists in other contexts and have also been applied to government and business organizations, without it, it seems, any recognition that the meanings and their social values may have changed somewhat

For example, these labels were used in experiments conducted in an informal classroom setting using 11-year-old boys as subjects. The descriptive labels applied to the climate of the setting as well as the type of leadership practiced. When these labels were transferred to a management setting, it seems that many presumed that they principally meant the king of leadership rather than climate. We can see that there is a great difference between the experimental and management settings and that leadership practices for one might be inappropriate for the other.

It is doubtful that formal work organizations can be anything but authoritarian, in that goals are set by management and a hierarchy exists through which decisions and orders from the top are transmitted downward. Organizations are authoritarian by structure and need; direction and control are placed in the hands of a few in order to gain fast and efficient decision making. Now this does not mean to describe a dictatorship. It is merely the recognition of the fact that direction of organizational affairs comes from above. It should be noted that leadership in some natural groups is, in this sense, authoritarian.

Granting that formal organizations have this kind of authoritarian leadership, can there be a democratic climate? Certainly there can be, but we would want to define and delimit this term. A more realistic meaning of democratic climate in organizations is the use of permissive and participatory methods in management-employee relations. That is, a mutual exchange of information and explanation with the granting of individual freedom within certain restricted and defined limits. However, it is not our purpose to debate the merits of authoritarianism versus democracy. We recognize that within the small work group there is a need for freedom from constraint and an increase in participation in order to achieve organizational goals within the framework of the organizational movement.

Another aspect of climate is best expressed by this familiar, and true, saying: actions speak louder than words. Of particular concern to us is this effect of management climate on the behavior of supervisors, particularly in employee-centered activities.

There have been reports of disappointment with efforts to make supervisors ore employee-centered. Managers state that, since research has shown ways of improving human relations, supervisors should begin to practice these methods. Usually a training course in human relations is established; and supervisors are given this training. Managers then sit back and wait for the expected improvements, only to find that there are none.

If we wish to produce changes in the supervisor's behavior, the climate must be made appropriate and rewarding to the changed behavior. This means that top-level attitudes and behavior cannot deny or contradict the change we are attempting to effect. Basic changes in organizational behavior cannot be made with any permanence, unless we provide an environment that is receptive to the changes and rewards those persons who do change.

IMPROVING SUPERVISION

Anyone who has read this far might expect to find *A Dozen Rules for Dealing With Employees* or *29 Steps to Supervisory Success*. We will not provide such a list.

Simple rules suffer from their simplicity. They ignore the complexities of human behavior. Reliance upon rules may cause supervisors to concentrate on superficial aspects of their relations with employees. It may preclude genuine understanding.

The supervisor who relies on a list of rules tends to think of people in mechanistic terms. In a certain situation, he uses *Rule No. 3*. Employees are not treated as thinking and feeling persons, but rather as figures in a formula: Rule 3 applied to employee X = Production.

Employees usually recognize mechanical manipulation and become dissatisfied and resentful. They lose faith in, and respect for, their supervisor, and this may be reflected in lower morale and productivity.

We do not mean that supervisors must become social science experts if they wish to improve. Reports of current research indicate that there are two major parts of their job which can be strengthened through self-improvement: (1) Work planning, including technical skills, and (2) motivation of employees.

The most effective supervisors combine excellence in the administrative and technical aspects of their work with friendly and considerate personal relations with their employees.

13

CRITICAL PERSONAL RELATIONS

Later in this chapter we shall talk about administrative aspects of supervision, but first let us comment on *friendly and considerate personal relations*. We have discussed this subject throughout the preceding chapters, but we want to review some of the critical supervisory influences on personal relations.

Closeness of Supervision: The closeness of supervision has an important effect on productivity and morale. Mann and Dent found that supervisors of low-producing units supervise very closely, while high-producing supervisors exercise only general supervision. It was found that the low-producing supervisors:

- check on employees more frequently
- give more detailed and frequent instructions
- limit employee's freedom to do job in own way

Workers who felt less closely supervised reported that they were better satisfied with their jobs and the company. We should note that the manner or attitude of the supervisor has an important bearing on whether employees perceive supervision as being close or general.

These findings are another way of saying that supervision does not mean standing over the employee and telling him what to do and when and how to do it. The more effective supervisor tells his employees what is required, giving general instructions.

COMMUNICATION

Supervisors of high-production units consider communication as one of the most important aspects of their job. Effective communication is used by these supervisors to achieve better interpersonal relations and improved employee motivation. Low-production supervisors do not rate communications as highly important.

High-producing supervisors find that an important aid to more effective communication is listening. They are ready to listen to both personal problems or interests and questions about the work. This does not mean that they are *nosey* or meddle in their employees' personal lives, but rather that they show a willingness to listen, and do listen, if their employees wish to discuss problems.

These supervisors inform employees about forthcoming changes in work; they discuss agency policy with employees; and they make sure that each employee knows how well he is doing. What these supervisors do is use two-way communication effectively. Unless the supervisor freely imparts information, he will not receive information in return.

Attitudes and perception are frequently affected by communication or the lack of it. Research surveys reveal that many supervisors are not aware of their employees' attitudes, nor do they know what personal reactions their supervision arouses. Through frank discussion with employees, they have been surprised to discover employee beliefs about which they were ignorant. Discussion sometimes reveals that the supervisor and his employees have totally different impressions about the same event. The supervisor should be constantly on the alert for misconceptions about his words and deeds. He must remember that, although his actions are perfectly clear to himself, they may be, and frequently are, viewed differently by employees.

Failure to communicate information results in misconceptions and false assumptions. What you say and how you say it will strongly affect your employees' attitudes and perceptions. By giving them available information, you can prevent misconceptions; by discussion, you may be able to change attitudes; by questioning, you can discover what the perceptions and assumptions really are. And it need hardly be added that actions should conform very closely to words.

If we were to attempt to reduce the above discussion on communication to rules, we would have a long list which would be based on one cardinal principle: Don't make assumptions!

- Don't assume that your employees know; tell them.
- Don't assume that you know how they feel; find out.
- Don't assume that they understand; clarify.

20 SUPERVISORY HINTS

1. Avoid inconsistency.
2. Always give employees a chance to explain their action before taking disciplinary action. Don't allow too much time for a "cooling off" period before disciplining an employee.
3. Be specific in your criticisms.
4. Delegate responsibility wisely.
5. Do not argue or lose your temper, and avoid being impatient.
6. Promote mutual respect and be fair, impartial, and open-minded.
7. Keep in mind that asking for employees' advice and input can be helpful in decision making.
8. If you make promises, keep them.
9. Always keep the feelings, abilities, dignity and motives of your staff in mind.
10. Remain loyal to your employees' interests.
11. Never criticize employees in front of others, or treat employees like children.
12. Admit mistakes. Don't place blame on your employees, or make excuses.
13. Be reasonable in your expectations, give complete instructions, and establish well-planned goals.
14. Be knowledgeable about office details and procedures, but avoid becoming bogged down in details.
15. Avoid supervising too closely or too loosely. Employees should also view you as an approachable supervisor.
16. Remember that employees' personal problems may affect job performance, but become involved only when appropriate.
17. Work to develop workers, and to instill a feeling of cooperation while working toward mutual goals.
18. Do not overpraise or underpraise, be properly appreciative.
19. Never ask an employee to discipline someone for you.
20. A complaint, even if unjustified, should be taken seriously.

NOTES

www.ingramcontent.com/pod-product-compliance
Lightning Source LLC
Chambersburg PA
CBHW081825300426
44116CB00014B/2486